The Tarahumara Rebellion of 1690

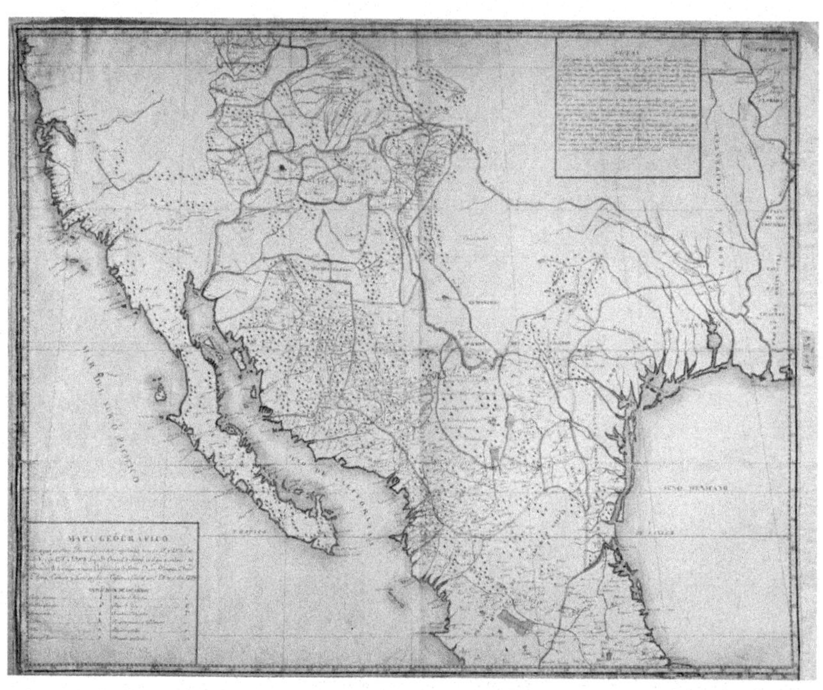

Manuel Mascaró's map of New Spain, 1779. Spanish Colonial Research Center Cartographical Collection, University of New Mexico.

JOSEPH P. SÁNCHEZ

The Tarahumara Rebellion *of* 1690

Embattled Settlers and Missionaries in Northern New Spain

THE UNIVERSITY OF
ARIZONA PRESS
TUCSON

The University of Arizona Press
www.uapress.arizona.edu

We respectfully acknowledge the University of Arizona is on the land and territories of Indigenous peoples. Today, Arizona is home to twenty-two federally recognized tribes, with Tucson being home to the O'odham and the Yaqui. Committed to diversity and inclusion, the University strives to build sustainable relationships with sovereign Native Nations and Indigenous communities through education offerings, partnerships, and community service.

ISBN-13: 978-0-8165-5585-7 (hardcover)
ISBN-13: 978-0-8165-5584-0 (paperback)
ISBN-13: 978-0-8165-5586-4 (ebook)

Cover design by Leigh McDonald
Cover art: Mapa jesuita del Noroeste de la Nueva España a mediados del siglo XVIII, courtesy of Manuel Orozco y Berra Map Library
Typeset by Leigh McDonald in Warnock Pro 10.5/14 and Bennett Display

Publication of this book is made possible in part by support from the UNM Center for Regional Studies. Special appreciation and gratitude is extended to Dr. Lloyd Lee, director of the Center for Southwest Research, University of New Mexico, for granting additional funding for both the publication of this book and its index.

Library of Congress Control Number: 2024060670

Printed in the United States of America
♾ This paper meets the requirements of ANSI/NISO Z39.48-1992 (Permanence of Paper).

For

Loretta, Brenilda, Helen, Anna, Tom, Joseph, Paul, and Kiki

CONTENTS

ACKNOWLEDGMENTS

Special thanks to the staff at the following archives: Archivo General de Indias, Seville, Spain; Archivo General de la Nación, Mexico City, Mexico; Archivo Histórico de Parral, Parral, Mexico; Archivo Histórico Nacional, Madrid, Spain; Biblioteca Nacional de Antropología e Historia, Mexico City, Mexico. Particularly, appreciation and thanks to my wife, Loretta Sánchez Sandoval, for her timely critique of segments of this study.

The Tarahumara Rebellion of 1690

INTRODUCTION

A Parallax View

From the earliest Indian resistance to Christopher Columbus's expedition to the Caribbean in 1492, to the last major outbreak of Native–white violence in North America at Wounded Knee in 1890, Indigenous people were, for all intents and purposes, at war with all foreign or alien intruders onto their homelands. Throughout the Americas, Native tribes fought against all trespassers, both European and Indigenous, to defend their land, resources, and people. The Europeans viewed such Native resistance as unjust rebellions or the treacherous revolt of savages against their legitimate sovereign. That legal position conflicted with the Native view that their wars, when undertaken, were a just struggle against European invasion and a righteous defense of their homelands. Perhaps Chiricahua Apache leader Geronimo said it best in 1905 when he met President Theodore Roosevelt. Explaining why he fought to protect his homeland, Geronimo began with "Great Father," the traditional greeting to a recognized authority or divine figure. He continued: "Did I fear the Great White Chief? No. He was my enemy and the enemy of my people. His people desired the country of my people. My heart was strong against him. I said he should never have my country."[1] Geronimo's words echoed the belief of all Native tribes that had resisted or battled imperial and colonial invaders, including those from the United States, since 1492.

Similarly, the Tarahumara rebellions throughout the seventeenth century were not only a continuation but a part of the overall Indigenous struggle for defense of homeland against all intruders that was replicated by thousands of tribes throughout the Americas. For centuries prior to the arrival of Europeans, tribes all over the Americas had defined their boundaries along river valleys, forest lines, mountains, ravines, and other topographical features of their land. Any crossing into their territory by other tribes was considered a hostile act. In prehistoric times, tribes honored topographic boundaries belonging to other tribes. Clearly, trespassing by other tribes onto their lands without permission was unwelcomed. By the middle of the sixteenth century, Indian tribes throughout the Americas were at war with intruding Spanish, English, French, Portuguese, Dutch, and other European invaders and their Native allies who assumed sovereignty over their territorial domains.[2]

The Europeans based their ownership of lands claimed by them by dint of discovery as a part of the domain owned by their sovereign kings. European sovereignty was the basis of claims by Spain, France, Portugal, England, and other powers. Beyond the early Spanish foothold on the Caribbean established by Columbus's first four voyages of discovery between 1492 and 1502, the fall of the Aztec Empire in 1521 began the Spanish sovereign claim to lands in North America.

Within the historical process, acts of possession were performed and documented by Europeans in the name of their respective kings. European claimants not only presented signed affidavits that such acts had been taken; they also issued land grants to settlers with titles such as *mercedes* (Spain), charters (England), *seignueries* (France), Patroon land tracts (Dutch), and *seismarias* (Portugal). Similarly, the Louisiana Purchase also violated Indian territorial traditions by falsely claiming that those lands stretching from the eastern edge of the Appalachian Mountains, beyond the Mississippi River, and across the Great Plains to the Pacific Northwestern coastline had been legitimately purchased from France.[3] The Great Plains Wars ensued for decades to validate such a claim against Indian territorial ownerships that had existed for hundreds of years. Oddly, almost unconsciously, the Louisiana Purchase appeared as a right to claim Indian lands between the Mississippi River and the Pacific Coast as the United States was the sovereign, in effect, and possessed a document that the land had been purchased and Indians had no rights to their claim. Assumed sovereignty, in European minds and historical legal traditions, justified such actions. Indian uprisings were the response.

Notably, treaties between France, Spain, and England in the early 1760s stated that Indian boundaries marked by rivers would be respected. But such attitudes were short-lived. Following the breakdown of the Proclamation Line of 1763, American frontiersmen pushed beyond the Appalachians to the Mississippi River without regard to Indian lands. Indian Removal became the policy under the United States and it spread with the Great Plains Wars of the nineteenth century. Thus, all European and American powers that trespassed on Indian lands justified their actions based on documented historical sovereign claims.[4] In the end, land occupied by Native tribes for thousands of years throughout the Americas was usurped by foreign sovereign powers.

Following the conquest of Tenochtitlan by Hernán Cortés in 1521 and the establishment of Spanish sovereignty over Aztecan imperial lands, Spanish exploration fanned out in all directions of the newly established Mexico City. Once silver was discovered north of Mexico City, a new pathway, El Camino Real de la Plata, the "Silver Road," as it was called, pointed soldiers, miners, settlers, and missionaries northward to Indigenous lands in Mexico's central corridor between the Sierra Madre Oriental and the Sierra Madre Occidental. There, European sovereignty tested the strength of Indigenous territoriality.

In 1530, Nuño de Guzmán undertook to conquer the area known as the Gran Chichimeca because of the many tribes that occupied a large area within Mexico's central corridor, which encompassed lands inclusive of present Chihuahua, Zacatecas, Durango, Torreón, San Luis Potosí, and Guanajuato. Administratively, a large part of that area became known as Nueva Galicia. That land, it was believed, held rich gold and silver deposits. Within that area lay many tribal lands, particularly those of the Tarahumara. In time, the Provincia de Nueva Vizcaya was carved from the large area once known as Nueva Galicia. During the last decades of the sixteenth century, wars were waged against Spanish settlers by tribes living within that territorial extension as far north as Chihuahua and New Mexico.

Indeed, the Tarahumara or Rarámuri, as they called themselves, were among the tribes that following the fall of Tenochtitlan and the discovery of silver near Guanajuato were at war with European intruders and their

Nahua allies in defense of their homeland. From 1540 to 1542, the Tarahumara, the Acaxee, the Tepehuan, and other tribes engaged Spanish forces and their Nahua allies in the Mixton War in Nueva Galicia.

Notwithstanding the occurrence of rebellions throughout northern New Spain, Spanish officials must have realized that the rebellions were not isolated cases. After investigations following each rebellion, as they occurred within each province of New Spain, they realized that such rebellions were part of a larger picture. The historical examination of the Tepehuan Revolt of 1616, for example, hinted that some Native rebellions were linked to events elsewhere in northern New Spain. Sixty-four years before the Pueblo Revolt of 1680, the Tepehuan Revolt of 1616 began in November in Sinaloa, south of Tarahumara country. While the Tepehuan warriors' well-planned assault sent settlers, miners, and missionaries scurrying for safety, all but destroying the Jesuit mission system in their homeland for several years, Spanish officials found that there were outside influences for the rebellion, including that of an Indian from New Mexico who had urged the rebellion. During six decades of warfare, many men, women, and children died on both sides, as large-scale destruction took place. The Tarahumara, the Tepehuan, and other tribes in northern New Spain held tight to their convictions regarding intrusions onto their lands. They had also strived to drive out intruders from their homelands.

By the early seventeenth century, missionaries had entered lands inhabited by the Tepehuan and the Tarahumara. As in all cases throughout the Americas, missionaries believed in the work they did to spread Christianity and save souls. Native Americans differed in such efforts and responded in many ways. Their leaders rejected Christianity and entire tribes were never Christianized. Only a small percentage of Natives were converted during the Spanish colonial period. Yet a syncretic set of beliefs and practices evolved among tribes within mission fields across the Americas. Aside from their own religious convictions, Native objections varied for their rejection, which usually ended in rebellion against the missionization process.

In his book, Father Andrés Pérez de Ribas, who wrote about the missionary efforts among the Tepehuan and the Tarahumara in the early seventeenth century, presented the complexity related to religious syncretism that existed in the minds of missionaries and Native peoples. In one example, among many issues related to tribes rejecting Christianity, he wrote about a particular problem some missionaries faced when a group refused to participate in daily church activities. One priest wrote of a certain incident when he "set out for another ranchería because he had learned that those who lived nearby had never wanted to go into the church. He gathered the people together to find out the cause of their rebelliousness and found that they were dissuaded by the fear that they would not be safe inside what they called the house of the dead. They gave this name to the church because they saw dead Christians buried there."[5] Over time, such clashing religious-based issues plagued the missionization program throughout the Americas.

Indeed, while religious issues were part of the dissonance between missionaries and Native peoples, the main overriding reason for rebellions dealt with tribes objecting to the presence of Spanish missionaries, settlers, miners, traders, and soldiers and their Indian allies who trespassed on and occupied their land. That issue was repeated many times, not only over Spanish-claimed lands but also throughout the occupation of other European colonial territorial claims.

Pacification of Native tribes, on the other hand, was the objective of the Spanish Crown. Spanish authorities used missionaries to pacify particular areas without the use of arms. Usually missionaries were sent to certain lands before settlers and other investors could occupy an area. In many cases, missionaries were among the first Europeans in far outreaches of the New World. Their presence among tribes was not welcomed. The Native American and the European views were always in conflict. The history of rebellions between 1540 and 1700 by Tepehuan, Tarahumara, and other tribes in Nueva Vizcaya as far north as New Mexico attests to the Native defense of homeland.

Father Andrés Pérez de Ribas, furthermore, reviewed early missionary efforts among the Tarahumara. Indeed, he wrote that missionaries worked two mission fields in Nueva Vizcaya, particularly those of the Tepehuan and the Tarahumara, who, linguistically different, were often at war with one another: "because our common adversary who reigned in these nations is also the enemy of peace, he always sowed discord between these peoples who engaged each other in wars and assaults."[6] Father Pérez de Ribas was referring to the "devil" as the common adversary who also afflicted the missionary effort.

TABLE 1 Rebellions in Nueva Vizcaya, 1540–1700

1540–42	Mixton War: Tarahumara, Tepehuan	Nueva Galicia
1540	Tiguex War (Coronado Expedition)	Albuquerque Valley
1565	Opatas resist Francisco de Ibarra	Sonora
1599–1601	Ximene	NW. and W. Durango
1599	Acoma	W. New Mexico
1601	Jumanos (sporadic warfare)	New Mexico
1601–3	Acaxee	NW. Durango, Topia
1610	Ximene	W. and NW. Durango
1613	Acoma	New Mexico
1616–18	Tepehuan, Tarahumara, Acaxee	W. and NW. Durango
1621–22	Tarahumara, Tepehuan	W. and E. Durango
	Tobosos and Conchos	S. Chihuahua
1630s	Tobosos, Tepetucanes, Salineros	Durango and Masames, Chihuahua
1644–75	Pueblo rebellions	Socorro, Jemez, Cochiti, Nambe, San Felipe, Isleta, etc.
1645–52	Tobosos, Conchos, Tarahumara	E. and NW. Durango, SW. Texas, N. and S. Chihuahua
1660s	El Tanbulita Rebellion: Salineros, Conchos, Tobosos, some Tarahumara	S. and NE. Durango, S. and W. Chihuahua, SW. Texas, New Mexico
1670s	N.M. Pueblos and Clemente Revolt	New Mexico
1680–1700	Pueblo Revolt (1680): Conchos, Tarahumara, Chizos, Sumas, Mansos, Tanos, Tobosos, Julimes, and Opatas	New Mexico, Sonora, Chihuahua, Durango, Texas

Source: Joseph P. Sánchez, "Indigenous Territoriality and European Sovereignty in the Early Centuries of European Discovery of and Claim to North America," New Mexico Historical Review 95, no. 2 (Spring 2020): 225–26.

Of the Tarahumara mission field, Pérez de Ribas noted that their "rancherías were well hidden and farther inland."[7] He also noted that the Tarahumara were easier to approach than were the Tepehuan, who were always ready to rebel. To missionaries, the Tarahumara seemed ready for missionization. Within the first decade of the seventeenth century, Father Juan Fonte had requested of the Father Provincial in Mexico City permission to establish a mission field among the Tarahumara. Father Fonte had entered Tarahumara country during the winter of 1607 and had noted that while the terrain was passable, he was told by local tribes in the area that

> other Tarahumara live in canyons where horses cannot cross. Many people dwell in caves that are plentiful in this land. Some are so spacious that they accommodated entire extended families; interior divisions of the caves are occupied by separate households. The men wear clothing consisting of mantas made from hemp, which is very well woven by the women, who also wear mantas of the same material. The women are very reserved and neither sit nor mix with the men. Their burial customs differ from other nations in that they have designated a separate place that is like a cemetery. They bury the dead with all their clothing and some food for the journey. The home of the deceased was burned or totally abandoned; relatives would mourn the dead by cutting their hair.[8]

While interest in a new mission field loomed, so too did violence between the Tepehuan and the Tarahumara in the area proposed by Father Fonte.

The establishment of the mission field was tenuous. Early on, Father Pérez de Ribas noted that "owing to certain fortunate or unfortunate events plotted by the devil . . . his goal is to impede the way to the Gospel and to disrupt the conversion of this nation's almost one thousand families. In spite of this, two of our priests who were sent from Mexico City for this enterprise are standing at the door and waiting to enter."[9] At that point, time stood on the threshold of a new phase for the missionization of the Tarahumara.

It seemed to Pérez de Ribas that the Tepehuan generally influenced coordinated rebellions against intruders and their allies. Following the Mixton War of 1540 and other succeeding events, for example, trouble had brewed among the Tepehuan and other neighboring tribes for many decades. Indeed, the heart of the Tepehuan homeland, known to be in the Valle de Guadiana in Durango, stretched northward astride the broad corridor of the Camino Real de Tierra Adentro from southern Chihuahua, Durango, and Zacatecas. Other lands within Tepehuan territory crossed onto other trails leading to Tepehuan lands in eastern Sinaloa and northern Jalisco and Nayarit.

During the intervening decades following the Tepehuan Revolt of 1616 and succeeding rebellions, the Tarahumara, who by 1690 planned to drive out Spanish miners, missionaries, settlers, and their Nahua allies, had learned much from the Tepehuan Revolt of 1616 and the Pueblo Revolt of 1680, which took place far to the north in New Mexico. On a broader scale, the Tarahumara not only knew about the Spanish refugees who had fled southward from New Mexico between 1680 and 1692 but watched, over those twelve years, troop movements in and out of New Mexico. In 1692, they observed the conquering army led by Governor Diego de Vargas march over the Camino Real de Tierra Adentro, which ran through their territory, to retake New Mexico.

At first, the reasons for rebellion appeared intangible as Spanish oppression was not evident among the Tepehuan as it was in areas affecting other tribes. It was determined by Spanish missionaries that the Tepehuan were very superstitious and were strongly influenced by their *hechiceros*, who to the Jesuits practiced a form of black magic. Seeing the Jesuit influence among their people, the *hechiceros* provoked rejection of the missionaries. Either jealous of the Jesuit influence or actually fearing what the missionary, settler, miner, and presidial soldier intrusion meant in regard to the destruction of their culture and way of life, they aroused their people to rise against them and drive them out.[10]

The Tepehuan Revolt of 1616 revealed yet another factor in their war to defend their territory. In the wake of the Tepehuan Revolt, the Spanish investigation regarding the causes of the revolt discovered a form of millenarianism in which local tribes believed that a messiah would return to organize and lead the Tepehuan to victory and rid their land of the invading Spaniards. That legacy pervaded future rebellions in Nueva Vizcaya.

It appeared that millenarianism had influenced the Tepehuan Revolt of 1616. Spanish officials and missionaries left behind a documentary dialogue concerning a strange visitation to the Tepehuan that likely inspired the revolt. In the official Spanish interrogatory that followed the rebellion, the Spaniards wondered if, in fact, during Lent of one of the previous years, an idol in the form of a badly formed cross had been carried by an Indian who traversed the land to incite them and who said that God had sent him to exhort them to rebel against and kill all the priests and Spaniards in the area. He said that all Indians killed in the rebellion would be "resurrected on the seventh day."[11]

Citing the "probanza," or interrogatory, made by fray Andrés de Heredia, guardian of the Convento de San Francisco in the Valley of Topia, on January 24, 1617, he noted the martyrdom of eight Jesuits and a Dominican who accompanied them. The interrogatory, furthermore, made at the request of Father Francisco Arista, S.J., who was president of the Colegio de Guadiana in Nueva Vizcaya, revealed that Father Heredia knew about an incident in which an idol in the form of a badly formed cross had been carried by a Tepehuan Indian who called for revolt. The interrogatory followed with a request for information regarding the message delivered by the Indian calling for the Tepehuan to rebel against the Jesuits and Spanish settlers. More importantly, the interrogator asked whether it was true that the referenced Indian had promised that "the Indians in the war once dead would be resurrected on the seventh day."[12]

The follow-up response to the interrogatory was chilling. Heredia, identifying Captain Martín de Olivas as the captor of the rebel Indians, had learned from them that the rebellion was instigated by an Indian from New Mexico who had, indeed, passed through several villages with a small crucifix with the figure of Jesus Christ. In the interrogatory that followed the Tepehuan Revolt, Captain Olivas's declaration revealed that captive Indians at La Sauceda had said that just before the rebellion an Indian had come from "la provincia del Nuevo Mexico and had, with another who translated for him, preached his insidious message. He carried a figure of the 'Cristo,' which was 'girded with a silk-like belt, and in it were two folded letters,'" both looking rather official. The two missives served as testimony, verifying that Christ was the "true son of God." The Indian also said that the son of God would descend from the heavens and would come "to visit and console them, and he would visit all of the world, particularly the poor people who were whom he loved throughout all of this land that the Spaniards had usurped and all they had served them as if they were their slaves."[13]

Olivas also said that the New Mexican Indian had told them that "God, the Father" had authored the letters telling them that abusive Spaniards and missionaries were corrupt and that the time for change was nigh. He exhorted them to rebel against the Spaniards and drive them out. He said that God had told them to rebel many times before; this time, if they did not do it, he would "destroy them and cast them into the fires [of hell]."[14] The New Mexican Indian explained that the two letters contained that message from God. He exhorted his listeners to select the wisest man among them to carry the Christ and the two letters from one pueblo to the next, preaching the message, until they reached the settlements at Guadiana. Before long, he had a large following.[15]

After a ritualistic ceremony revolving around the Cristo and the two letters, the New Mexican Indian left the area. Later, the messianic message surfaced in small rebellions of other tribes in Nueva Vizcaya. Thus the seed for a rebellion, coordinated by certain leaders in various pueblos, was planted. Many of the warriors in the region began by constructing and stockpiling bows, arrowheads, and shafts for the coming rebellion.

Later in his history, published in 1645, the Jesuit priest Andrés Pérez de Ribas confirmed that there was, indeed, an influential person who fanned the flames of rebellion. Pérez de Ribas wrote that "a sorcerer" made several disguised apparitions among the Tepehuan, Acaxee, and Xixime nations exhorting them to rebel.[16] Attributing the rebellion to the devil and his lying ways, Pérez de Ribas wrote that when an old Indian

> entered the pueblos of Santiago, Tunal, and Tenerapa, which were all near Durango, he preached perversely against our Holy Faith, with the harmful intention of inciting those people to abandon their Faith and rebel against God and the king.... He told them that this was the God whom he and his companions worshiped. Afterwards, however, he went to the aforementioned pueblo of baptized Tepehuan, called Tenerapa, which was not far from Santiago Papasquiaro. There he ordered that his idol be worshiped, and through his lies and tricks he convinced these Indians that both he and his idol were angry and offended because he had assigned the Spaniards a homeland in kingdoms on the other side of the ocean in Spain, and yet they had come to these parts without his permission, settling in his lands and introducing the Christian law. He wished to free them of this, and in order to do so, as well as to placate their true gods, they would have

> to cut the throats of all long-time Christians, particularly the priests and fathers who instructed them, as well as all the Spaniards in the region. . . . If they obeyed him, he promised them safety for their own lives, their women and children, and victory over the Spaniards. Even if some of them should die in battle, he promised them that within seven days they would be resurrected.[17]

The elements of the story were repeated in other testimonies of the period.

The sojourn of the New Mexican Indian left a lasting imprint on the Tepehuan. Eventually the Tepehuan developed a philosophic premise that formed a legacy within their culture and theology. They firmly believed, through their evolving seventeenth-century ceremonies and rituals, that a recurring theme reinforced their conviction that the "true savior is the *tlacatexista* or 'Cristo'" that they had carried with them from pueblo to pueblo as the New Mexican Indian had charged them to do. They had learned well that the Cristo had come to their land to look after them as they suffered tyranny and exploitation by Spaniards. Even though the Jesuits had taught them about the "Cristo," they nonetheless viewed them as members, or at least supporters, of the exploiters. They adopted the "Cristo" as their own into their religious ideologies and formed their own beliefs that the "Cristo" had come to save them.[18] Indeed, in at least one way, the broader story came full circle: from the defense of ancestral lands and the honor of the spirits of their ancestors, their descendants found a way to sustain their way of life through a useful syncretic union of old and new beliefs. While "millenarianism" would appear philosophically profound, the historic survival of the tribes depended on both war that worked as a short-term solution and surrender that was an initial phase of the long term.

Again, the Tarahumaras and the Tepehuan battled with trespassers onto their land between 1616 and 1618. Between 1621 and 1622, the Tarahumara, Tobosos, Conchos, and Tepehuan attacked Spanish settlers, Nahua allies, miners, and missionaries in Durango and in southern Chihuahua. Between 1645 and 1652, Tobosos, Conchos, and Tarahumara waged war against Spanish settlers in a large area from eastern and northwestern Durango to southwestern Texas and Chihuahua. By 1660, a large rebellion of Tarahumara, Salineros, Conchos, and Tobosos, hoping to drive out the intruders, widened their area of attacks to southern and northeastern Durango, southern and western Chihuahua, southwestern Texas, and southern New Mexico. The large Tarahumara revolt began sporadically in 1685 and blew into full-force warfare in 1689 and 1690. During that period extending between 1680 and 1700, Tarahumara, Chizo, Suma, Manso, Tano, Toboso, Juileme, Opata, and New Mexican Pueblo warriors individually struck a wide area in Sonora, Texas, New Mexico and most of Chihuahua, and Durango. While Spanish officials labeled each engagement as an isolated "revolt" or "rebellion" against Spanish sovereignty, assuming that the tribes were part of the Spanish sovereign body, the tribes viewed their attacks as a defense of homeland against intruding Spanish settlers, miners, missionaries, and their Indian allies.[19] Yet, such violent conditions did not deter missionaries, settlers, miners, and ranchers from going there.

Much had been learned about the people and land of Nueva Vizcaya during the colonial period. Those who settled the area knew that, aside from warring tribes, the land, in certain areas, was forbidding, ranging from hot to cold weather patterns. Indeed, the land varied in its climate. In the late seventeenth century, Father Joseph Neumann, a Jesuit missionary in Nueva Vizcaya, noted weather patterns in the mountainous and arid lands of Chihuahua. He described the rains that came in June and wrote that it would rain all month, until the feast day of John the Baptist on June 24. The rest of summer was dry. Then, from November to February, it was very cold, with snow that sometimes fell two to four times a day. From March and April until the middle of May, the weather varied. High winds were so strong that dust storms blocked the sun.[20] Such was how the weather fluctuated throughout the year in earlier times.

Today, the Chihuahua Desert (Desierto de Chihuahua) ecoregion is a hot desert and semiarid region. With its extended geographic influences, the Chihuahua Desert lies in effect within the following coordinates: 30°32′26″ N, 103°50′14″ W. Covering a large area of about 193,783 square miles, it is considered to be the largest desert in North America. Largely it consists of mountain ranges, basins, and river valleys. The Chihuahua Desert ecosystem has evolved within the past eight thousand years.[21]

The Chihuahua Desert includes two large mountain ranges with the perfect nicknames, as said in English, "Mountain Mamas": the Sierra Madre Occidental to the west and the Sierra Madre Oriental to the east.[22] The range and boundaries of the Chihuahua Desert include parts of northern Mexico and the southwestern United States. Its far-reaching geographical extents include portions of Arizona and Texas as well as southern New Mexico. In the west it is bordered by the Sonoran Desert, the Colorado Plateau, and the Sierra Madres. Throughout the desert scape, a variety of flora is evident. Yuccas, creosote bushes, and tarnish dominate the northern and western portions of the Chihuahua Desert. Herbaceous plants such as bush mutely, blue gramma, gypsum drama, lechuguilla, and ocotillo as well as varied agave and grasslands are common throughout the area.[23] Common fauna include the Mexican gray wolf; a variety of amphibians, lizards, and snakes; pronghorn, javelina, jaguars, cottontails, and kangaroo rats; eagles, hawks, Peregrine falcons, owls, and other winged species; and butterflies, beetles, wasps, scorpions, and other insect species.[24]

Another aspect is the heritage of the tribes that today continue to carry on ancient traditions in a modern world. Today, as in the past, the main Indigenous tribes in Chihuahua are Tarahumara, Tepehuan, Nahua, Guarijío, Mazahua, Mixtecos, Zapotecos, Pimas, Chinatecos, and Otomí. Today, the Tarahumara, Tepehuan, and other tribes live under the Republic of Mexico. Despite the push to acculturate into the mainstream culture, the Tarahumara, Tepehuan, and other tribes have retained their Native languages and cultural heritages.

CHAPTER 1

SELECTED HISTORIOGRAPHICAL LITERATURE ON THE TARAHUMARA REBELLIONS

Historiographically, much has been written about the Tepehuan and the Tarahumara as well as about those in surrounding tribes, which, throughout the seventeenth century, between 1608 and 1697, waged continuous warfare against intruding missionaries, settlers, miners, and soldiers, along with their Tlaxcalan allies.[1] For nearly ninety years, the Tepehuan, Tarahumara, and their allies hoped to rid their traditional lands of the Spanish intruders and their Nahua allies, who not only occupied their lands but also attacked their cultural norms as well as their spirit world.

Much has been written about the various Tarahumara rebellions in the seventeenth century as well as the Spanish missionary, mining, settlement, and military efforts in Nueva Vizcaya. Historiographically, most of it is repetitive in terms of known details, as such publications are in the form of chapters or sections in books or article-length studies published in scholarly journals. The following historiographical summary, moreover, notes examples of selected publications regarding the referenced history in relation to rebellions, settlements, missions, and mining interests in Nueva Vizcaya. Such writings demonstrate the historiographical pathway historians have taken in dealing with the Tarahumara and Tepehuan rebellions of the seventeenth century that continued into the eighteenth century.

The first known account of the Tarahumara rebellions in the seventeenth century was written by Father Joseph Neumann around 1724.[2] In his recollections and knowledge of Nueva Vizcaya, where he served as a Jesuit missionary to the Tarahumara, he recounts nearly ninety years of Tepehuan and Tarahumara rebellions. His work is a large anchor in the historiography of the Tarahumara rebellions.

In the eighteenth century, the Jesuit and historian Andrés Cavo wrote *Historia de México*, which was published in 1836.[3] He was among the Jesuits who were expelled from New Spain in 1767. His book, written as an apology for the Jesuit Order, was an early attempt to write a historical account about the Spanish domination of Mexico. Historiographically, Father Cavo was one of the first historians to write about the Tarahumara rebellion of 1689–90.

Among the early American historians to write about the Tepehuan and Tarahumara rebellions was Hubert Howe Bancroft.[4] His account, published in 1884, features the early history of Nueva Vizcaya and the Tepehuan and Tarahumara rebellions. Although the information in his accounts of both rebellions appears outdated, the influence of his writings set a historiographical pattern of how that history would be treated and repeated by future writers. Still, the information in the Bancroft account has value historiographically as new documentary sources added to the clarification of the tumultuous history of Nueva Vizcaya in the seventeenth century.

Bancroft covers topics dealing with the Jesuit missions in Tepehuan country and rebellions tied to them, particularly the later Tarahumara uprisings. In reviewing the 1616 Tepehuan uprising, Bancroft seeks to examine the reasons behind it, pointing to a pattern of cultural preservation as well as the defense of homeland. Even though the Jesuits had reported to Spanish officials in Durango that there was an uneasiness among the Tepehuan, their warning went unheeded. Still, from the Jesuit point of view, as Bancroft points out, the lack of support from the governor in Durango was a large part of the Tepehuan Revolt of 1616. Usually the Jesuits blamed settlers and minors for the disturbances leading to violence, but this time, as Bancroft, using the writings of seventeenth-century Jesuits, points out, the ill feeling came from the surrounding tribes. *Hechiceros*, or sorcerers, hoping to preserve their spirit world, clashed with the Christian God.

Of such dissidence, Bancroft, looking at the initial reason for the outbreak by the Tepehuan, examines the case regarding the flogging of a certain *hechicero.* He writes: "All the more earnestly after his flogging, but also with more caution did this Tepahuane messiah continue his teachings, bearing always with him an idol and claiming the two, by some kind of mysterious duality, were God, and angry that without his consent the Spaniards had crossed the ocean. No more were to be allowed to come, and all here must be killed, especially the missionaries."[5] Bancroft's historical analysis repeats information presented in the writings of two seventeenth-century Jesuits, Father Joseph Neumann and Andrés Pérez de Ribas. In regard to a particular *hechicero,* in 1645 Father Pérez de Ribas writes that there had indeed been an influential person who had fanned the flames of rebellion. He says that "a sorcerer" had made several visits to the Tepehuan, Acaxee, and Ximime tribes, exhorting them to rebel and take back their homeland.[6]

Twentieth-century writers have built their studies around the earlier Jesuit presentations of Nueva Vizcaya, the Tarahumara and Tepehuan rebellions, and the history of Jesuit and Franciscan missions that served the various tribes in the seventeenth century. In the twentieth century, Joaquín Ramírez Cabañas, in 1940, edited *Descripción geográfica de los reinos de Nueva Galicia, Nueva Vizcaya y Nueva León.*[7] In this documentary description of the missions in Nueva Galicia, later known as Nueva Vizcaya, Ramírez Cabañas presents another view of the missions and missionaries in Tepehuan and Tarahumara country during the sixteenth century. Looking through the eyes of Bishop Alonso de la Mota y Escobar, Ramírez Cabañas adds to the historiographical and biographical literature of the missionaries in Nueva Vizcaya and the missions they served. Bishop de la Mota, who in his *visita* surveyed the missions, presents a view of Nueva Galicia as the Camino Real and mining ventures expanded into Tepehuan and Tarahumara lands. He also expanded information on the settlement patterns within the growing province.

Still another view of official Spanish policies regarding the tribes in the area is explored in Roberto Mario Salmón's writings, as he wrote a survey and analyses of Indian rebellions in northern New Spain for the period 1680 to 1786. In so doing, he reviews Spanish Indian policy that grew out of the late seventeenth century as well as relationships between Spaniards, mestizos, and Native Americans in Mexico's northern frontier that included Nueva Vizcaya; New Mexico; Sonora, Coahuila, and Sinaloa; Texas; and Baja and Upper California. In his 1991 study, Salmón focuses on Indian rebellions as responses to pressures on tribes made by encroaching missionaries, settlers, merchants, miners, soldiers, and their Indian allies as well as free Black slaves and mulattoes.[8] Salmón notes that at every situation, northern tribes, in particular, faced threats revolving around encroachments on their lands, political jurisdictional claims by Spanish officials and missionaries, and challenges to their cultures. In that regard, Salmón's study adds to the historical roundtable regarding tribes in northern New Spain that rebelled to save their territorial claims and cultural heritages and beliefs.

Similarly, in her book published in 1992 for the quincentenary commemoration of Columbus's first voyage, Ysla Campbell details the history of early contact made by Spaniards with various tribes and cultures in northern Mexico.[9] Her book briefly recounts known aspects of the Tarahumara rebellion. Still, her documentary probes regarding the Jesuit missionary venture in Mexico add to the historiographical knowledge of missionary contacts with the various tribes in Mexico.

In their analyses of documentary sources, Ernest J. Burrus, S.J., and Félix Zubillaga examine sixty-eight documents that pertain to the northern frontier of New Spain between 1600 and 1789.[10] The documents largely regard the Jesuit missionary efforts among the Tarahumara in Nueva Vizcaya as well as the histories of New Mexico, Sinaloa, Sonora, and California. In it, they disclose five documents dealing with the Tarahumara in the seventeenth and eighteenth centuries. Such a study adds knowledge offered by firsthand accounts of life in Nueva Vizcaya in the first century and a half in a large geographic area.

Modern-day Jesuits continued to write histories of the early missionary efforts in northern Mexico. Father Peter Masten Dunne, S.J., for example, wrote about the early Jesuit missionaries among the Tarahumara. His 1948 book includes chapters on the Jesuit missions that focus on the seventeenth century.[11] Hoping to support his analyses with historical documents found in Mexican archives, such as those in Parral, Chihuahua, Dunne studies official Spanish colonial perspectives to the events of the period. He notes that the 1607 silver rush into Nueva Vizcaya began the intrusion of miners, missionaries, settlers, soldiers, and Spanish officials onto Tepehuan and Tarahumara territories. He also chronicles the successes and failures of the early missionaries in the area, namely the Jesuits. To that end, Dunne includes the travails of Father Neumann, who in the seventeenth century worked with the Tarahumara and struggled with their continuous resistance to his and other Jesuit efforts. As explained by other historians, he accounts for the cyclical and sporadic uprising by various tribes over intrusions into their lands and cultures. Dunne introduces one more step in the jurisdictional rivalries between clergymen and officials. His study contributes to the historiography of the Tarahumara and Tepehuan rebellions and shares similar details found in other studies. Indeed, other studies, by Jesuit historians and colleagues, broaden the storyline by expanding their studies to a broader history of the Jesuit experience in Mexico.[12]

Luis González Rodríguez's book about the Tarahumara, while largely historical, includes contemporary accounts of Tarahumara culture and society. The study contains chapters regarding evangelization efforts by Jesuits and Franciscans between 1604 and 1767. In this work, González Rodríguez includes information about Indigenous rebellions, destruction of missions, massacres of civilians and missionaries, destruction of Spanish settlements, and mines as well as brutal Spanish reprisals. Parts of his study are based on the account by Jesuit Father Joseph Neumann.[13]

In 1979, Thomas E. Sheridan and Thomas H. Naylor edited a documentary collection that pertains to aspects of Tarahumara history. The Rarámuri, as the Tarahumara are also called, are the subject of a selected fifteen Spanish colonial documents largely written by seventeenth- and eighteenth-century Jesuit and Franciscan missionaries. The documents deal with life in the missions; conflicts with Spanish officials, settlers, and miners that resulted in rebellions; and issues dealing with Native territoriality and European sovereignty over their homeland.[14]

A part of the historiography of Nueva Vizcaya is an important documentary collection that also includes the Tarahumara uprisings.[15] Edited by Thomas H. Naylor and Charles W. Polzer, S.J., the collection consists of reports, journals, correspondences, and policies of military officials involved in the Chichimec War in Nueva Galicia (1576–1606); rebellions in the Sierra Madre Occidental (1601–18), and repositioning of fortifications in New Spain (1640–60) as well as documentation on rebellions that occurred between 1681 and 1695 on the northern frontiers. While it focuses on military aspects of New Spain, it includes one section on

Spanish colonial relationships with the Tarahumara and their succeeding rebellions.

Other modern-day historians continue to write about the Tarahumara and Tepehuan rebellions, adding new perspectives yet rewriting accounts mentioned in earlier historiographical studies. One important study, however, written by Susan M. Deeds documents missions, primarily Jesuit missions, and the difficulties confronting the missionaries in Nueva Vizcaya during the seventeenth and eighteenth centuries.[16] Deeds recounts the labor policies enforced by Spaniards on Indian laborers in mines and on haciendas. Deeds explains the rivalry among Jesuit missionaries and Spanish officials in Nueva Vizcaya regarding Indian labor. The Jesuits, as explained by Deeds, added to the resentment among the Tarahumara when they tried to restrict Native cultural practices and meddle with their spirit world. On that subject, Father Neumann, himself a Jesuit, notes that the intensity of violence against the Jesuits was greater than that against Franciscans. To that, Bancroft surmises that in general, Natives found the Franciscans to be more tolerable than the Jesuits.[17]

Perspective was added to the history of the administration of Jesuit missions by Father Charles W. Polzer, S.J., in 1979, when he sought to define the efforts of Jesuit missionaries beyond the realm of expansionism. He writes about rules and regulations within the process in the founding and the administration of the mission. In one instance describing the establishment of a mission, he writes that in

> the earliest stages of evangelism a missionary decided on an Indian village as his mission of residence. Other Indians of the same tribe would be invited to live at this village; sometimes they were forcibly brought to the chosen village so they could be systematically exposed to the process of cultural change. Once a village was designated as a cabecera [headquarters], there was still no guarantee that the headquarters mission for that partido would always remain there. . . . Missionaries who opened up new regions frequently selected their visits as sites for future cabeceras. . . . The *visita* is most commonly a mission station at a smaller Indian village or ranchería. But the term itself, in mission literature, also has broader applications, as when a whole mission province is described as a "visit" in relation to the Father Visitor . . . relative to the administrator visiting.[18]

Thus, the mission, from a missionary point of view, required more than attempting to acculturate or teaching them about the faith; it was about establishing a residence, which required Indian labor, within an Indian community where—aside from the conversion process, which was his ultimate goal—he would spend a great deal of his time in supervising the establishment of farmlands or the construction of a church.

As in all other histories written about the Tepehuan and the Tarahumara, who resisted acculturation efforts by the missionaries, the basic premise among the tribes in Nueva Vizcaya, as well as throughout the Americas, was that the European encroachment by Spanish settlers, miners, missionaries, soldiers, and their Indian allies on their lands was not wanted or tolerated. In her study, Deeds, as did Bancroft, also discusses the effect of rampant epidemics in the missions.[19] Those issues led to rebellions that occurred throughout the seventeenth century and spilled into the eighteenth century. With each uprising, the Tarahumara receded further into the sierras and the deep canyon recesses of the Sierra Madres to avoid contact with the Europeans and all that it implied.

The historiographical writings on the Tarahumara–Tepehuan rebellions are reflected in a myriad of articles and chapters in books. A sampling of such articles is provided to reflect the historiographical representation in the form of scholarly dialogues on the subject. For example, Deeds reiterates her findings on the Tepehuan and Tarahumara uprising against the missionaries in Nueva Vizcaya. In her study, in this case a chapter in a book on Latin American missions, Deeds focuses on a historiographical perspective of the province of Nueva Vizcaya and the Native American responses to the missionaries' efforts to convert them.[20] She relates the history of Spanish intrusion onto their lands as mines, missions, settlements, and presidios were established. Deeds repeats the historiographical tenets made in earlier publications regarding tribal defense of homeland as well as other causes for the rebellions. She also notes the alliances formed between the Tarahumara, Conchos, Acaxee, Xixime, Tepehuan, and other tribes in the area. Deeds stresses that the missionization of the Tarahumara failed to change their culture. Still, the Tarahumara did adapt to certain aspects of Spanish culture, such as learning the Spanish language, raising livestock, farming, and becoming horsemen, all influenced by Spanish settlement of the area. Deeds's focus, nonetheless, as she had in her earlier publications, adds publications to the history of the Tarahumara rebellions.

Allan Christelow's 1939 journal article, on the other hand, reflects the earlier historiographical tempo. In it, he presents a comprehensive history of the Tarahumara based on his study of Father Neumann's life among the Tarahumara. While there is little new in this article, historiographically it is part of the scholarly interest in adding new speculations about the rebellions in Nueva Vizcaya.[21]

As in his book-length publication, Roberto Mario Salmón, in his 1977 article on the Tarahumara rebellion against Jesuit missionization, recounts the efforts by both missionaries and settlers who sought to Europeanize Indians while expanding onto their lands and establishing mines, ranches, and farms.[22] Salmón again notes the abuses suffered by various tribes at the hands of miners, soldiers, and settlers as well as the attacks on their spirit world by missionaries. He discusses the issue of how Spanish missionaries, miners, and settlers rejected, as superstitious, the Indian spirit world and the leadership of their *hechiceros*. The result, as he writes, was a series of uprisings that aimed to force Spanish intruders off their lands. Salmón stresses the brutal attacks made by the Tarahumara and their allies against miners, missionaries, settlers, and presidial soldiers. He also notes the brutal responses made by armed Spanish settlers, miners, and soldiers. While Salmón stresses the seventeenth-century rebellions, he explains the failure of the Tarahumara rebellion of 1690 as well as the continuous warfare in the following century.

While there are other articles written on the subject of seventeenth-century Indian rebellions in Nueva Vizcaya, these three sources are representative of the historiographical efforts made not only to reveal the history of such rebellions but also to review aspects of the historical process that brought about such changes throughout Nueva Vizcaya as well as representing the history of European expansion throughout the Americas, Africa, and places like Australia.

Key Places in Nueva Vizcaya

Nuevo Mexico x
x
x El Paso del Norte
x
Janos x
x
VALLE DE PAPIGOCHI x
Villa de Aguilar x
Papigochi Chihuahua
S S
I I
E Yepómera x E R
Cushuiriachic x R
R x R
A Balleza Parral A
Santa Barbara
Sonora Guazapares x M
M x
A x A
D x D
R x R
E Zape x E
x
O Papasquiaro
x x O
C x x R
C x Cuencamé I
I x E
D x N
E x x T
N Durango x A
T x L
A x
L
Sinaloa Zacatecas x
Camino Real de Tierra Adentro x
x Mexico City

Key places in Nueva Vizcaya. Geographical schematic compiled by the author.

CHAPTER 2

SPANISH SETTLEMENTS, MISSIONS, AND MINES ALONG THE CAMINO REAL DE TIERRA ADENTRO IN THE SIXTEENTH CENTURY

At the beginning of the historical era, the Native American homeland in Chihuahua comprised a great number of divergent tribes, subtribes, and bands of Indians, which were culturally and linguistically complex. Some were nomadic; others were sedentary. Some dwelt in hot desert lands, while others lived in high, cooler mountain ranges of the Sierra Madre Occidental and the Sierra Madre Oriental. They lived by hunting and by foraging within the flora and fauna of the area. Others lived in the more tropical recesses of the barrancas and farmed corn and other foodstuffs in clearances and along river banks. Once Spaniards came into the area, many tribes adapted by raising herds of cattle and sheep. They quickly adapted to becoming horsemen, an integral part of a rapidly changing Indian world.[1] In Chihuahua, as elsewhere throughout the Americas, tribes such as the Tarahumara and their allies commonly deplored the invasion of their lands by Spanish, English, French, Portuguese, Dutch, and German sovereigns, among others.

The complexity of Spanish settlements, laws, practices both governmental and ecclesiastical, as well as cultural heritage and sense of purpose was much more unexpected than the mere presence of settlers, miners, and missionaries. Beyond the sovereign claim made on behalf of the Spanish king, explorers traversed the Americas looking for valuable resources that ranged from salt deposits, spices, and dyes to water sources, farming lands, hard- and softwood forests, as well as mineral wealth in terms of copper, iron, tin, silver, and gold. In so doing, they, using Indian pathways, developed trails that crisscrossed the land leading to certain places. Such authority, for Spaniards, either to explore or to settle an area, was done only with privilege granted to do so by the sovereign or his representative, namely, the viceroy. Legal documents for exploration included contracts that were issued specifying not only the area to be explored; once at the site, the explorers also prepared signed legal affidavits by those present verifying that a reading of the sun had been taken confirming that the latitude and longitude of the area in question had been taken and claimed for Spain.

By the middle of the sixteenth century, Spaniards had explored much of Mexico from the Atlantic to the Pacific coastline and had mapped and developed trails connecting new settlements, missions, mines, ranches, and farms. Some roads, with fortifications on them, were protected trailways, known as *caminos reales*, or Royal Roads. The longest of the four *caminos reales* in New Spain was El Camino Real de Tierra Adentro (Royal Road of the Interior), which ran nearly 1,600 miles of a meandering trail, from Mexico City to Santa Fe in New Mexico. The other three ran from Mexico City to Veracruz, Acapulco, and Honduras.

The historical development of protected roads is part of the Greco-Roman tradition with roads such as the Appian Way. The definition of a *camino real* in accordance with Spanish colonial law and practice, moreover, is paramount in understanding the significance of *caminos reales* throughout the Americas and their origins. The legal sources regarding *caminos reales* are found in compilations or codes of laws and policies that followed Spanish practice and tradition. From tradition, shaped from Greco-Roman times, sprang a body of laws that formed the legal practice and jurisprudence of Spanish America.

The antiquity and dynamics of tradition and practice regarding the administration of *caminos reales* and settlements are found in the *Fuero Juzgo, Fuero Real,* a codex of laws compiled in medieval Spain in 1241. The laws of the *Fuero Juzgo* passed to the modern age through the *Nueva Recopilación*, the *Recopilación de las Leyes de los Reinos de las Indias*, and the *Novísima Recopilación de 1805.*[2] It is clear from these laws that privileges were extended only to individual Spaniards or associates of

Spaniards, primarily of the Peninsular and Creole social classes. Colonial minorities performing the business of the king benefited from certain privileges, especially if they were prescribed in contractual form.

Associated with *caminos reales*, settlements, ranches, farms, missions, presidios, and other geographic points are trails that connected them, such as those in Nueva Vizcaya, and which were recorded in Spanish colonial cartography. Under the Laws of the Indies, the settlement of lands was done under contract with the sovereign or his designees. Similarly, military units and fortifications were governed by statutes in the Laws of the Indies that prescribed military "*reglamentos*," as did missions under the "Patronato Real."

After 1600 and before 1700, the presidial line followed the settlement pattern along the Royal Road as it turned northeast toward El Pasaje, then zagged northwest to El Gallo, south of Mapimí, then northerly to Cerro Gordo south of Parral and the presidio of Conchos north of there. Before the century ended, the northernmost garrison was at El Paso and a militia, composed of male settlers, was at San Gabriel in northern New Mexico.

Along with presidios, settlements were established along the Camino Real. Accordingly, all was done in compliance with the Laws of the Indies. Under Spanish colonial law, the authority to establish settlements with the right to govern was given under Spanish law once thirty settlers or ten married men with their families established the minimum population.[3] Additionally, the boundaries of each settlement were marked as part of the process defined in laws governing land grants. Thus, the act and process of settlement and claim were strictly accomplished in accordance with law, practice, and tradition.

Indeed, throughout the Americas, Spanish laws aimed to protect lands owned by peaceful Indians living in villages. Despite the fact that tribes considered the Spanish presence within their territorial lands an intrusion, Spanish law prohibited settlers from crossing into or occupying tribal village lands. Under the Laws of the Indies, Spain strived to respect Native American lands. Settlers and officials, for example, were not allowed to live in Indian pueblos, not allowed to buy Pueblo lands, not allowed to graze livestock on Pueblo lands, and not allowed to have livestock ranches within eight miles of a Pueblo mission. Also, the law stated that no ranches could be established near pueblos. It was also stipulated in the Laws of the Indies that any lands taken from Indians living on them must be returned to them.[4] Regardless of such legal sentiments, the issue remained: from the point of view of tribal territoriality, Spanish settlers, miners, missionaries, and traders were invaders and should be driven out.

Yet Spain's settlement of the Americas, as that by other European powers, would be unstoppable. The establishment of towns, cities, and other establishments such as missions, fortifications, ranches, mines, etcetera, was so ordained by European sovereigns. The historical process, from their point of view, had been moving forward since Columbus's first voyage.

In terms of establishing a body politic on each frontier area, the Spanish sovereign approved that governing bodies be put in place. Once a Spanish settlement was established, the Laws of the Indies required a representative governing town/city council, known as a cabildo, be established and prescribed that each town council would have an alcalde (mayor), four regidores, one sheriff, one scribe, and one mayordomo, totaling eight representatives.[5] The Laws of the Indies furthermore prescribed that alcaldes could not be reelected until a period of three years had passed, and cabildo representatives had to wait out a two-year vacancy.[6] Provincially, local cabildos oversaw observance of laws and policies emanating from the Laws of the Indies.

Aside from those in Nueva Vizcaya, Mexico's northernmost Cabildo de San Juan de los Caballeros (1598) and Cabildo de la Villa de San Gabriel (1599) were established in New Mexico. As with all cabildos throughout the Americas, the opening of the cabildo of 1603 at San Gabriel in New Mexico, for example, was made according to custom and prescribed procedures. Traditionally, in New Mexico, as in settlements in Nueva Vizcaya and elsewhere in the Spanish Empire, designated officials opened their town meetings by announcing its purpose and calling out the names of its officials. For example, the cabildo of San Gabriel of 1603 opened its meeting when the council clerk announced, "¡Sepan cuanto! Sepan cuanto!" (Know Ye . . . Know ye . . .) that the "Cabildo Justicia Regidores [Honorable Regents of the Cabildo] de la Villa de San Gabriel del Nuevo México stand together in this congregation of our cabildo, in accordance with custom and practices in common voice to deal with local affairs and fulfill the business of this town meeting." Then the council clerk announced the names of the officers of the council present: "Capitán Francisco Rascón, Alcalde ordinario [Ordinary Mayor of this Villa de San Gabriel] y Hermano de Hinojos, y Antonio Gutiérrez, y Gonzalo Hernández y Pedro Sánchez Monroy, y Juan de Medel, all Regents, empowered by El Señor Don Juan de Oñate, Governor, Captain General and Adelantado of this kingdom and province as authorized by the King of Spain. Power is accorded them under the auspices of the Cabildo de la Villa de San Gabriel."[7] Thus, each settlement throughout the Spanish Empire, in accordance with the Laws of the Indies, followed strict procedures in the proceedings of each cabildo.

Overall, the business of the cabildo was to attend to the res publica, the affairs of the people, by addressing issues within the province. The cabildo voted on policies in conformity with the Laws of the Indies on all matters that affected the town, colony, or province. Inescapable to the eye would have been the interactions of the cabildo with the people within the colonial society of a given place who presented testimony regarding the issues at hand. Beyond their social status, political leaders, the clergy, the laymen or the laity, itinerant traders, drovers, scribes, soldiers, and others in colonial societies seemingly had much in common as citizens of the empire.

Early in Spain's occupation of settlements throughout the Americas, cabildos had been established, particularly in provincial capitals.[8] The earliest cabildos designated as provincial capitals, for example, were established at Santo Domingo (Dominican Republic, 1496), which is the oldest European capital in the Americas. Other cabildos were established at Caparra, Puerto Rico (1508), Havana, Cuba (founded in 1518, official capital status in 1607), Mexico City (1525), San Agustín, Florida (1565), and, in New Mexico, San Juan de los Caballeros (1598), which was superseded as capital by the Villa de San Gabriel (1599); a decade later, the capital was moved to Santa Fe (1610). The cabildo at Parral was established in 1632. In each case, provincial capitals served, in their time, as terminals on Camino Real de Tierra Adentro.

In all cases, the legal concept applied to the fact that provincial capitals were the terminals of *caminos reales* as the trail passed through other settlements, on their way to capitals in other provinces. For example, in Nueva Vizcaya the *camino real* from Mexico City reached the provincial capital at Durango before proceeding northward to the provincial capital of Nueva Vizcaya at Parral and thence on to New Mexico's capital in Santa Fe. Generally, provinces were divided into districts with towns that had cabildos, which reported to the governor and cabildo at the provincial capital. *Caminos reales* did not go to Indian settlements as did spur trails emanating from *caminos reales*.

For all intents and purposes, a Spanish presence, beyond that of missionaries and soldiers, was established once settlers moved into an area, along with ranches and farms as well as opportunities for trade and the development of foodstuffs for soldiers and missionaries. Significantly, settlers introduced Spanish civil government into each area they settled. Such a presence troubled the tribes, who saw settlers as intruders onto their land.

Spanish settlements, therefore, were much more than settlers constructing their homes and establishing farmlands. Throughout the Spanish Empire, in places like Nueva Vizcaya, societal boundaries evolved that were tied to Spain's mission to spread Christianity and to establish governance, law, and associated institutions, as well as to occupy the land for whatever it could yield in agriculture, trade, or exploitation of resources.

Yet life in a Spanish settlement was filled with everyday occurrences and scenarios. Had one walked into a Spanish settlement with its plaza during the colonial period, for example, one would have heard the sounds of dogs barking, horses neighing, mules braying, along with those of cattle, goats, and sheep. At certain hours of the day, church bells made their clanging sounds announcing a moment of prayer. On a human scale, a given mix of people representing all colors—Spaniards, mestizos, Black and mulatto people, Indian allies—and all walks of life would have met the eye, and their voices expressing laughter, conversation, or heated discussions would have been heard at once. Spaniards, mestizos, mulattoes, Indians, and Asians, old and young, busily occupied the streets and markets within a given plaza.[9]

In the center of a town, a plaza housed the institutions of church and state. Their structures formed the vertical cultural landscape of a given place. Each town had its cabildo (town hall) and its chief politicians: the alcalde mayor and his regidores (regents) of the cabildo. From time to time, the governor of the province, as required by law, would tour the province and visit outlying settlements at least once a year.

Surrounding a given town, farmlands dotted the landscape with apple, peach, and apricot orchards as well as cultivated fields of melons, wheat, corn, chiles, and other assorted vegetables. Between the adjoining settlements were open ranges for pasturing herds of cattle, sheep, oxen, horses, and mules. In general, aside from stables or storage sheds for farm products, in corrals or within fences with small hutches near the homes of the settlers, one would have seen smaller numbers of domestic animals such as chickens, turkeys, milk cows, and goats, along with a few sheep and hogs for consumption. Farmlands with their attendant acequias (irrigation ditches) would have dotted the landscape along rivers. Outlying settlements would have been, according to the Laws of the Indies, located near such necessities as water, wood, and pasturage. Other food sources, as available, included fish, wild birds, and foraging mammals.[10] Prosperity was ephemeral in the settlements. While money poor, settlers lived by bartering what they produced off the land.

Near Spanish settlements or in faraway isolated places, missionaries established their churches and residences, sometimes, as did the Jesuits, within Indian settlements. They, too, were governed by a duality of agreements between Church and state known as the Patronato Real, in which the missions were subsidized and, to an extent, governed politically by the state. Beyond missionary involvement with tribes, Spanish authorities dealt with non-mission Indians. Usually, not far from the outskirts of Spanish settlements, were Indian settlements, some estranged or alienated from Spanish communities, who saw Spanish settlements as an invasion of their lands. Still, in some areas, Native settlements were similar to their Spanish counterparts, particularly farming communities. In distinct areas of the Spanish Empire were Indian farming communities. In other areas, there were rancherias or settlements of non-Pueblo tribes—in the case of Arizona, New Mexico, and Texas, for example, Opata, Sibubapas, Apache, Navajo, Ute, and Comanche communities—that lived off the land and trade.[11]

Spanish officials developed a dual Indian policy of dealing with peaceful tribes such as the Pueblos and the warring tribes, especially those who lived in Nueva Vizcaya or the eastern plains and woodlands north and east of New Mexico on the Great Plains and western Texas as well as in Sinaloa and Sonora, which affected both civil and religious entities. Spain dealt with the tribes as "naciones," or nations. Yet the dual Indian policy defined the "Gentiles," or those who had not yielded their sovereignty to Spanish authority, or those, like the Pueblos, who at least placated Spanish authorities by saying they accepted Spanish sovereignty. For them, coexistence was a means of survival. On the other hand, colonials preferred the object lesson approach rather than the destruction of Native groups.[12] Indeed, control of Native groups functioned as the preferred alternative. Groups or individuals who resisted coercion accordingly suffered the consequences of colonial European justice. Throughout the seventeenth century in Nueva Vizcaya, for example, the Tepehuan, Tarahumara, Tobosos, and other tribes, from time to time, acceded to Spanish force and authority for the sake of survival. Yet, from time to time, such tribes rebelled against Spanish sovereignty.

Settlements along a given *camino real* met with all kinds of challenges from surrounding tribes in their areas. One other element of life along a *camino real,* since the Laws of the Indies prescribed that such were protected roads, dealt with the positioning of military units to assure, as best as possible, protection of settlements and mines as well as missions that were off the main road. The locations of settlements, mines, forts, and missions determined the complexity of a given *camino real.* In his study, Philip Wayne Powell writes about the intricacies of the route from Querétaro to Zacatecas that eventually led north to Durango and Parral. Powell examines the principal settlements and stopping places (*parajes*) of the evolving Camino Real de Tierra Adentro as follows:

> Going north from Mexico City, the route of travel was already well defined as far as Querétaro by the time of the Zacatecas discovery. There was a regular traffic of merchants, officials, cattlemen, and livestock through this province of Jilotepec, a region that did not offer great travel difficulties. The principal settlements and stopping places for the traffic were Cuautitlán, Tepejí, Jilotepec, and San Juan del Río. Between Querétaro and the later foundation of San Felipe there were two main roads toward Zacatecas. One went northwest direct to San Miguel, then along the east bank of the San Miguel River toward San Felipe. The other went north from Querétaro passed just to the east of the Nieto Pass, where a road branched off to San Miguel, then turned northwest through Jofre Pass (near the later San Luis de la Paz), passing through the llanos called La Mohina, and joining with the other road at a point between the Río de los Sauces and San Felipe. The combined road then went north west through the portezuelo of San Felipe to Ojuelos. Just beyond Ojuelos it passed a point known as Encinillas,

> which was considered to be the dividing line on the Zacatecas highway between the audiencias of Nueva Galicia and Mexico. From Encinillas the road passed through Las Bocas and Ciénega Grande (both fortified by the viceregal government during the 1570s), then on to the paraje del Cuicillo, nine leagues from Zacatecas, where it joined another road going north from Michoacán.[13]

Given the locations of the places listed, distance was a factor as well as the location of water, firewood, and pasturage, all of which added to the complication that *caminos reales* were much more than a line on a map. To be sure, all common or public colonial roads, inclusive of spur trails in the Spanish domain, were protected roads, but the special distinction was given to large trunk trails that connected Spanish provincial capitals, ports, presidios, and villas to each other.

While the longest of the *caminos reales* in North America is the Camino Real de Tierra Adentro that ran from Mexico City to Santa Fe in New Mexico, its history is tied to that of Nueva Vizcaya. Thus, the tie between Nueva Vizcaya and New Mexico is a shared history as it relates to Spanish colonial expansion northward. Another *camino real*, an offshoot of the Camino Real de Tierra Adentro, departed Nueva Vizcaya, eastward, through Zacatecas and Cuencamé. It was known as the Camino Real de Tierra Afuera (Royal Road of the Exterior) as it ran toward the Gulf of Mexico via Saltillo. It connected to a series of segmented trails toward Texas with names such as the Camino del Río Grande, the Camino de San Antonio, and the Camino de los Tejas, which terminated at Los Adaes, the first Texas capital, located today near Robeline and Natchitoches in western Louisiana. Far to the west, along the Pacific Ocean coastline, the Camino Real de las Californias ran from Loreto by land and La Paz by sea on the east coast of Baja California. The land route ran west into the interior from Loreto to the western coast of Baja California via Velicatá and then due north to connect with the trail in Alta California that ran from San Diego to San Francisco. Similarly, there were many *caminos reales* throughout the Americas that comprised the Spanish Empire. Each *camino real* crossed through Indian homelands throughout the Western Hemisphere.

As with the legalities tied to settlement patterns, a long history of juridical definitions and practices, linked to Spanish legislation cited in the *Recopilación de las Leyes de los Reinos de las Indias,* defined the uses of a given *camino real* as intended by Spain. Aside from land routes, the use of maritime lanes, along coastal settlements of the Camino Real de los Tejas as well as the Camino Real de las Californias, in particular, are a part of the land routes that connected at ports and bays. Those routes are, indeed, a part of the Camino Real system for trade as well as migration.

As an emigrant trail in the sixteenth century, El Camino Real de Tierra Adentro traversed nearly the entire length of the interior of present-day Mexico to New Mexico through the Meseta Central between the Sierra Madre Occidental and the Sierra Madre Oriental. In time, it took on significance as the first step in the northward expansion of Spanish settlements and the development of a mining frontier. Indeed, *caminos reales* served as conduits in the expansion of European culture, language, religion, and folklore; economic institutions such as ranches, farms, mines, and trade companies; and music and cuisines common to the era.

Significantly, Indian pathways determined parts of the route of the Camino Real as its routing was modified by corridors that supported wagon trains, horses, mules, and cattle as well as the newly founded locations of settlements, missions, and mining areas.[14] All *caminos reales* throughout the Americas shared a common history based on legal precedents that originated in ancient traditions governing protected roads.[15]

The interior was the focus of enterprising Spaniards, once silver and gold were discovered north of Mexico City. The first phases of the march northward from Mexico City took place in the late 1540s as silver mines were discovered in Querétaro, Guanajuato, San Luis Potosí, and Zacatecas. The first silver rush, the first wagon trains of settlers, and the first cattle drives in North America took place along this trail. Indeed, the first forty-niners in North American history were those who rushed to the silver mines before the decade of the 1540s was over.

The establishment of Zacatecas in 1546 represented an important phase of the development of the trail as Spanish settlers pushed northward to other fields, thus expanding the settlement pattern beyond the Zacatecas–Durango frontier line. With expansion came demands for protection and pacification of the area. To that end, missionaries and soldiers moved forward to establish religious and military institutions along the route.

Mining throughout Nueva Vizcaya, whether in the central portion of the province or on the edge of the Sierra Madre Occidental, seemed a constant occurrence. In time, mines were being worked throughout Nueva Vizcaya, bounded by the present-day states of Chihuahua and Durango. Between the Sierra Madre Occidental and the Sierra Madre Oriental, the edges of the geographic expanse of Nueva Vizcaya, were many mines in out-of-the-way places with names like Batopilas, Parral, Guarisamey, San Dimas, Tayoltita, Gavilanes, Ventanas, Picacho, Cuencamé, Real de Oro, Mapimí, San Diego, Santa Bárbara, and Cusihuiriachi, among others.[16]

While early explorers looked for gold, they also sought other sources of mineral wealth such as copper, iron, and silver. Indeed, the Aztec silver mines at Taxco, south of Mexico City, caught the eye of early conquistadors around 1525.[17] As elsewhere, the opening of mines led to the establishment of settlements as well as missions and presidios. While gold had been discovered between Guanajuato and Zacatecas, north of Mexico, in the late 1540s, silver mining was the main source of wealth in seventeenth-century Nueva Vizcaya.

The discovery of mineral wealth that resulted in the opening of mines was governed by the Laws of the Indies, which called for fairness under the law, which was not always the case. For example, the laws prescribed that once mineral wealth, in this case gold, was discovered, the discoverer must appear before the governor of the province and personally declare that a discovery, whether along a river or in a backcountry area, was made and its estimated values to be reported to the Real Hacienda (Royal Treasury). In each case, the governor would issue a license to the discoverer to exploit the discovery and open a mine.[18] To assure that the Crown collected its *quinto* (known as the Royal Fifth, which was a royal tax of 20 percent) of precious metals discovered and mined, the Laws of the Indies stated that miners who discovered gold, silver, quicksilver, or other metals adhere to the law by assuring that those who worked the mines be paid as well.[19]

In order to discourage idle people from being hired, the laws also stipulated that under the watchful eyes of Spanish officials, Spaniards, mestizos, and Black and mulatto freedmen should be hired to work in the mines.[20] The laws also prescribed that those who labored in the mines could not sell any of the mineral wealth they gathered for the mine operator.[21] Above all, the laws prescribed that miners be favored. In so doing, the laws ordered viceroys, presidents, governors, town mayors, and justices throughout the Indies to favor the miners and quicksilver operators and that they be protected and their work not be impeded.[22]

Significantly, while one of the earliest silver strikes occurred near Guanajuato and opened El Camino Real de la Plata (the Royal Silver Road), the silver strike at Zacatecas in the late 1540s served as the cause for further expansion northward. Little by little, Spanish miners, ranchers, farmers, missionaries, and miners made their way northward. By 1549, the well-traveled road from Mexico City to Zacatecas attracted the attention of Viceroy Antonio de Mendoza as new roads from the agricultural fields of Michoacán, Guanajuato, and Querétaro developed to supply workers in the mines and missions that were being founded along the way.

The earliest silver discovery in Nueva Vizcaya may have taken place as early as 1547 in the vicinity of Santa Bárbara.[23] Within the next twenty years, the mining frontier in Nueva Vizcaya spread to an area between Indé in Durango and Santa Bárbara, far to the north.[24] By 1575, the frontier line had moved as far north as Santa Bárbara–Parral in present-day Chihuahua. There, the Tarahumara and their allies saw the first major movements onto their land. Presidios between Querétaro and Durango dotted the road and defined the importance of protecting the settlement pattern. For example, during the period 1570 to 1600, presidios between Querétaro and Guanajuato at Maxcala, Jofre, and Atotonilco marked the beginning of the route. Often they were preceded by missionaries who sought to convert the Natives to Christianity. Spanish officials also saw the missions as a way to pacify an area and open it to settlers and miners.

In that same period, the progression of the presidial line moved north of there to Jasó, Portezuelo, Ojuelos, Bocas, Ciénega Grande, Cuicillo, and Palmillas, reaching Zacatecas. Beyond Zacatecas, just south of Durango, the presidial garrisons at San Martín and Llerena for a while marked the northernmost end of El Camino Real de Tierra Adentro.

Spanish settlement in the sixteenth century reached into northern New Mexico. With the establishment of New Mexico by Juan de Oñate in 1598, the trail took a major jump from Santa Bárbara to the confluence of the Rio Chama and the Rio Grande, into the Pueblo world of New Mexico far along the northern Rio Grande.

In 1595, Viceroy Luis de Velasco and Juan de Oñate agreed on a formal contract for the settlement of New Mexico.[25] The settlement, while it opened a new frontier area in northern New Spain, was similar to the undertakings of other settlers throughout Nueva Vizcaya. All were done under a contractual agreement, in most cases known as a *merced*, or land grant. In this case, under the terms of the contract, which developed a history of its own owing to several disputes between Oñate and Viceroy Velasco, Oñate would pay all expenses for the expeditionary force, except for the Franciscan missionaries who were subsidized by the Patronato Real, a special fund for missionaries. In return for underwriting certain expenses, Oñate would receive a salary and hold the title of adelantado. Additionally, he would serve as governor and captain general in command of all troops within his jurisdiction, and he would administer the encomienda, a feudal collection of tribute from Indians under Spanish control. Generally, if Indians could not pay the tribute, the amount due was converted to payment in servitude. There, too, as elsewhere, Indians saw Spanish settlers as intruders onto their land. There were other provisions stipulated in his contract.[26] Even so, Oñate hoped to develop an inheritable, entailed estate (*mayorazgo*) from lands acquired in New Mexico.

On January 26, 1598, after much delay and great expenditure to Oñate, the expedition was permitted to leave for New Mexico. In a great cloud of dust, the slow-moving, oxen-pulled carreta caravan creaked out of the Valle de San Bartolomé in Nueva Vizcaya, in present-day Chihuahua, which also encompassed present-day Durango, a part of southwestern Texas, Sonora, and Sinaloa. Driving thousands of sheep, pigs, goats, cattle, mules, and horses, the soldiers and settlers began the trek to their new homeland far to the north. Scouts, led by Sargento Mayor Vicente de Zaldívar, nephew of Oñate, wandered far ahead of the wagon to find an easier route with water and pasturage.[27] As they approached the Rio Grande, light snow had fallen in the area as a cold wind swept the desert of northern Chihuahua. They reached the northernmost point of settlement near the pueblo called Ohkay Owingeh, which the settlers called the Pueblo of San Juan.[28] By 1599, the settlers had moved the capital from San Juan de los Caballeros, following regulations stipulated in the Laws of the Indies, to a place they called San Gabriel, at the confluence of the Rio Grande and the Rio Chama. There, the presence of missionaries, settlers, and soldiers was evident to Native tribes.

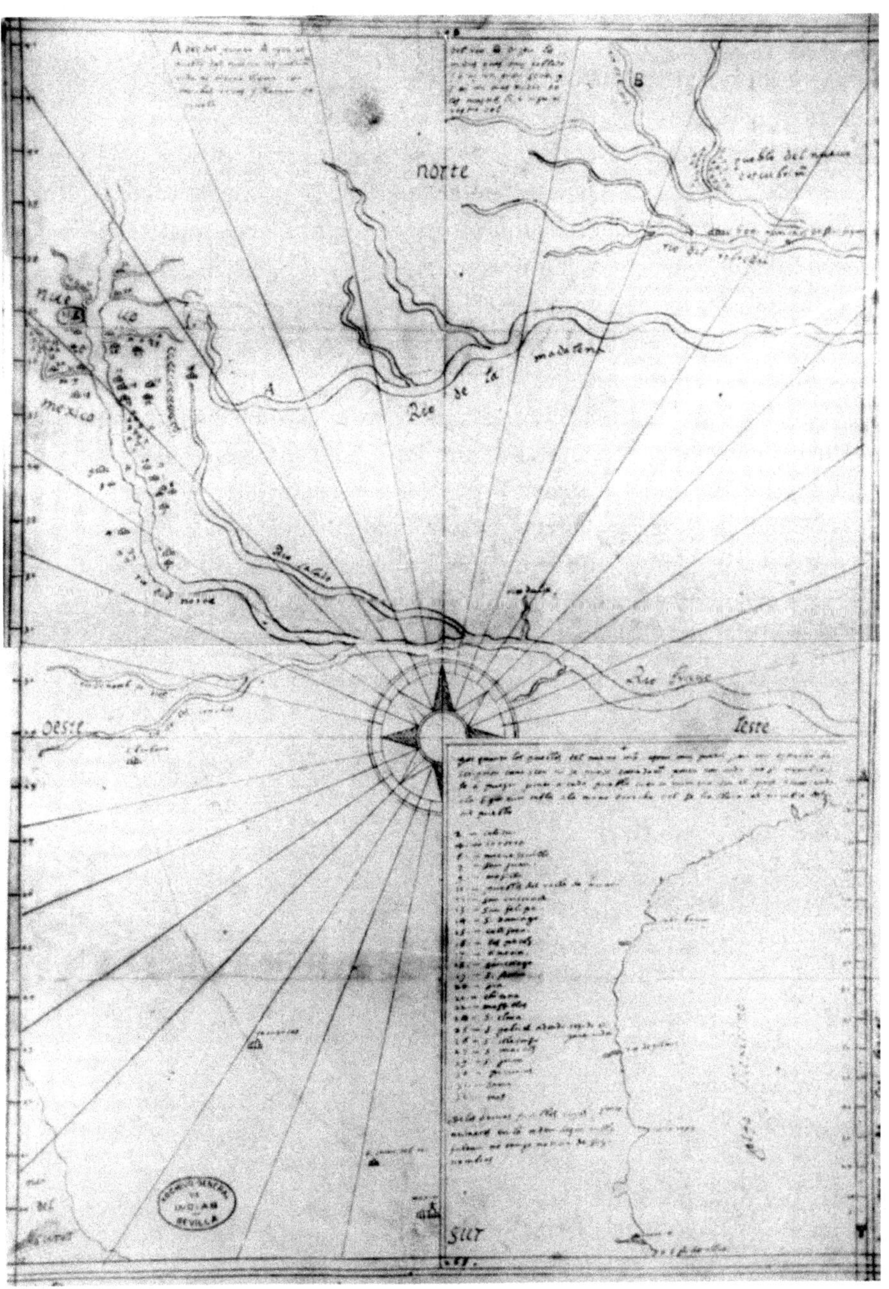

Map of the Camino Real through Nueva Galicia to New Mexico during Juan de Oñate's expedition of 1598. Map by Enrico Martínez, 1602. Center for Southwest Research Collection, Zimmerman Library, University of New Mexico.

Spanish frontiersmen depended on the presidial line to defend their properties. They also depended on missionaries to pacify areas near their settlements. Land grants, estancias, farmlands, and other estates specifying land tenure developed along the Camino Real. By the end of the seventeenth century, a new definition operated along the Royal Road. The word *hacienda,* which once meant moveable property, such as harvest and livestock *haciendas,* now extended to include specialized properties with mills for mining purposes.[29] The mill, animal driven or water powered, characterized the harvest and processing of minerals at mining haciendas. The words *mill* and *hacienda* became virtually interchangeable. Along the Camino Real, countless mills were constructed and, because of their economic importance, became associated with place-names along the route. In time, haciendas with mills were associated with extensive landholding patterns characterized by large fortified houses. So impressive were certain haciendas that they became towns on the Camino Real. Travelers on the Royal Road depended on haciendas for shelter and protection. Still, the surrounding tribes rightfully saw Spanish colonial progress as an invasion of their land and a threat to their way of life.

CHAPTER 3

SPANISH SETTLEMENTS, MISSIONS, AND MINES ALONG THE CAMINO REAL IN THE SEVENTEENTH CENTURY

Warily, and angry at such blatant intrusions onto their traditional lands, tribes bided their time, for they knew well the locations of their enemies. Throughout Nueva Vizcaya, presidios, missions, haciendas, mines, and frontier settlements dotted the land off and on the route of the Camino Real.

For nearly sixteen years, movement into Nueva Vizcaya appeared slow. In 1632, fueled by mineral wealth possibilities in the area, more than three hundred miners and settlers ventured northward along the traces of the Camino Real and founded San José de Parral, which served as a gateway to the reestablishment of Nueva Vizcaya. The establishment of San José de Parral on the Camino Real de Tierra Adentro proved to be an overpowering event to the tribes in the area, for, as the headquarters of both political and military administration, it demonstrated that the Spaniards were there to stay. Before long, Jesuit and Franciscan missionaries were back, working among more peaceful and sedentary groups. Soon, other missionaries, as it was their place to work among the unconverted tribes, would be assigned to that land.

Within five years the north was reinhabited by Spanish farmers, cattle ranchers, and miners who founded new settlements as far north as the Río Florido and the Conchos. Places like San Diego, the Villa Escobedo, and San Bartolomé were established in Nueva Vizcaya. Before long, more than twenty Jesuit and Franciscan missions dotted the area. The Jesuits worked among the Tarahumara scattered within the canyon lands of the Sierra Madre Occidental.[1]

For Spanish settlers in Nueva Vizcaya and northward along the Camino Real, life took on several themes. Beyond the discontent of warring tribes regarding Spanish settlers' intrusions onto their land, there were other occurrences demonstrating the volatility and violence on the frontier in all quarters. Issues of law and order among their own kind pervaded the settlements. Such themes were interconnected in a complicated frontier that included events such as the discovery of mineral wealth, namely silver; fear of Indian attacks on settlements and mines; and the malicious intents of men who sought to discourage others from mining in the area.

Although the story of Nicolás de Aguilar may seem to be an exception, it nonetheless indicated the fluidity of life on a rigorous and violent frontier between Nueva Vizcaya and New Mexico. Aguilar, for example, was a laborer in a mine in Nueva Vizcaya. He was born in 1623 of mestizo parentage and was reared at Yuriripundaro in Michoacán.[2] He said he had lived with his mother until he was eighteen years old, when he moved to Parral in southern Chihuahua.

Aguilar first came to the attention of Spanish officials in 1641 after claiming that jumpers had caved in his mine.[3] The teenaged frontiersman appealed to the *justicia mayor*, Juan Soltero Francisco, to bring charges against four men: Sebastián de la Canal, Diego Jiménez, Alférez Alonso García de Cárdenas, and Pedro Gonzáles. Apparently, these men had entered Aguilar's mine, which was located on land owned by Juan Gutiérrez at Real de San Diego, and pulled down a supporting pillar, collapsing the mine in the hope of intimidating the young miner to abandon his claims. Aguilar stated that his mine was seventy-two feet deep (six *estados*) and that among other minerals, he was mining for iron. Justicia Mayor Soltero brought charges against the marauders and found in favor of Aguilar.[4]

For the next thirteen years, nothing is heard about Aguilar until a fateful night in mid-February 1654. Then, his life took a different turn. On the eve of Ash Wednesday of that year, García de Cárdenas, one of the perpetrators against Aguilar in 1641 and now captain and *alcalde mayor* of the Real de Minas de San Diego, was awakened by a loud knocking on his door. It was late at night, about ten o'clock, and García's servants scurried in the dark, fumbling for their lanterns. Outside could be heard the sound of men's voices. "Come and do the business important to the service of the king," shouted one of the men to García. When García opened his door, he was greeted by an angry Hernando de Villagomez, mayordomo of the mines and uncle to Nicolás de Aguilar.[5]

Villagomez complained that Aguilar had forcibly taken his daughter, his daughter-in-law, and the wife of Nicolás Aroche to a hideout in nearby hills. Without hesitation, Captain García organized the men into a posse of eight Spaniards and eight Indians and followed a trail to the place where Aguilar held the women.[6]

From his hideout, Aguilar could see the orange-yellow light of torches used by the posse men as they came up the hill, some on horseback, others on foot. Suddenly, from behind a large boulder, he appeared before them. Heavily armed, he pointed an arquebus at the men. In the faint light, they could see that he carried two other arquebuses, one slung and the other in his left hand. He shouted some words at Captain García. The intrepid García shouted back that Aguilar was a thieving dog (*perro ladrón*) and ordered him to "give himself up to the law." Words were exchanged between Aguilar and his uncle. Aguilar fired his weapon and withdrew into the darkness.

Before anyone had realized it, Hernando de Villagomez lay dying from a wound to his forehead. From atop a large boulder, Aguilar held the posse at bay as the man's life ebbed from him. Realizing something terrible had happened, two of the captured women came from behind a boulder. Upon seeing her father dying, one of the women begged Aguilar to let someone get a priest, but he refused. Villagomez died that night in southern Chihuahua. The last any of them knew of Aguilar was the sound of his horse galloping into the night. The next day, Captain García and his men tried to find his trail but failed.[7]

Years later, in 1663, Aguilar told his version of the shooting. He said his uncle had gone "with the men to kill him." According to Aguilar, Villagomez fired first with a musket, but his weapon misfired; the spark hit the pan (*cazoleta*) but did not ignite the powder. At that instant, Aguilar returned fire and killed him. He said he escaped with only the shirt and a pair of white trousers he wore that night. Aguilar explained that after he had served the king for eight of ten years, he had been pardoned by the governor of Nueva Vizcaya.[8] Actually, he was confused about the *indulto,* for Governor Bernardo López de Mendizabal of New Mexico stated that Aguilar had taken advantage of a *cédula de indulto,* a royal pardon, issued by the king on the occasion of a prince being born to the royal family. The *cédula de indulto* granted a general amnesty throughout the empire.[9]

As Aguilar had entered New Mexico during the administration of Governor Juan de Samaniego y Jaca (1653–56), Governor López vouched that he had satisfactorily proven himself as an able and loyal soldier and citizen. During the late 1650s, Aguilar, a large man, served as a soldier, like most frontiersmen in the category called men-at-arms. As *sargento* and adjutant in the Villa de Santa Fe, probably under Governor Samaniego, and later as inspector (*visitador*) of the trade carreta caravans of Andrés de García, who lived at the bend of the Rio Grande near present El Paso, Aguilar earned his way into the graces of New Mexican administrators.

Sometime during this period, he married Catalina Márquez, granddaughter of Gerónimo Márquez, one of the pioneering settlers who had come to New Mexico with Juan de Oñate in 1598.[10] Nicolás and Catalina raised a family of four children.

In 1659, Governor López, upon the recommendation of Governor Juan Manso and the former governor Juan de Samaniego, appointed Aguilar as *alcalde mayor* of the jurisdiction of Las Salinas. Given their view of a brash and ruffian frontiersmen, the Franciscan missionaries there called him "the Attila of New Mexico." Aguilar was tried by the Holy Office of the Inquisition and exiled from New Mexico.[11] Spanish officials had traced Nicolás de Aguilar from Michoacán, to Nueva Vizcaya, to New Mexico, and finally, to his exile in Mexico City. Thus, the fluidity of life on such a rugged frontier as that of Nueva Vizcaya showed how quickly life could change on a mining frontier that was open to violence at all turns.

Meanwhile, settlers, miners, and missionaries in Nueva Vizcaya focused their attention on the Valle de Papigochi. Jesuits worked an area in Tarahumara and Tepehuan country eighty leagues long and sixty leagues wide. The Tarahumara met them with friendship. When the settlers came, they settled within the wide area and established settlements in uninhabited land.[12] During the administration of Governor Diego Guajardo Fajardo, settlers, around 1649, saw open land in the Valle de Papigochi, about seventy leagues from Parral. There, they established a settlement called Villa de Aguilar, where they built their homes, settlements, pasturelands, and farmlands, where they mostly planted wheat in the area. While they opened trade with the Tarahumara, they hoped to find silver within the area they had settled. In effect, many settlers were miners as well. To protect their farms, ranches, settlements, and mines, the settlers, much to the dismay of local tribes, built a bastion, or defensive tower, garrisoned by soldiers.[13]

During that time, Jesuit missionaries began working in the area. They, too, had petitioned Governor Guajardo Fajardo to establish a garrison for their protection. The Jesuits centered their work among the Tarahumara in the Valle de Papigochi. One of their first missions was at Teméchi, about ten leagues from Guajardo Fajardo's presidio.[14] The mission at Teméchi was the first mission to be attacked.[15] Attacks made in 1632 were led by a fierce leader named Cobamea, who also attacked the settlement at Chínipas.[16] Those early mission sites were abandoned and not worked by Jesuits between 1652 and 1673.[17]

Still, other issues dominated relationships between missionaries, settlers, miners, and soldiers as well as the Tarahumara and their allies, who, now tired of war, wanted peace. As had occurred during the administration of Governor Guajardo Fajardo, the presence of soldiers and the exploitation of Natives in mines was resumed, as was the diligent watchful eyes of resentful tribes, who watched the new intrusion onto their lands.[18] By the 1640s, miners were back in control of their mining domains. The mining frontier in Chihuahua resulted in the exploitation of Indian laborers who were forced to carry on their shoulders heavy silver-laden rocks and other debris in rawhide bags up pole ladders in overheated conditions.[19] Those and other issues led to fierce outbreaks led by Tepehuan, Tarahumara, and their allies.

Other issues that were the cause of rebellion were the mission and its religious issues that virtually condemned the Indian spirit world. Despite the ministering words of the padres, resentment and hatred spilled into violence in Parral in May 1646. Once again, Spanish settlements and missions, along the Camino Real and other pathways west and north, exploded into violence.

As events occurred along the Camino Real, they were noted by travelers. One of the earliest observers along the route in the first decades of the seventeenth century, Bishop Alonso de la Mota y Escobar, chronicled many occurrences and developments as he toured the newly reestablished Nueva Vizcaya. He himself, a contemporary of such events, was born within the first generation of settlers in Mexico City.[20] Dedicating himself to the Church, Bishop de la Mota y Escobar had spent his life as a clergyman, and became bishop of Guadalajara in 1597. Later, in 1606, he was appointed to the bishopric of Puebla, where he served until his death in 1625.[21] Following an Indian uprising at Topia in Nueva Galicia in 1601, de la Mota y Escobar, as bishop of Guadalajara, undertook a pastoral inspection of the province. With his known zeal, he traveled extensively throughout Nueva Galicia, which later became Nueva Vizcaya, and recorded from his detailed notes his *Descripción geográfica de la Nueva Galicia.*[22]

Through the eyes of Bishop Alonso de la Mota y Escobar, one is able to see how life on the linear frontier of the Camino Real operated as Spain expanded its effective claim deeper and deeper into the interior of New Spain in the late sixteenth and early seventeenth century.[23] The development of the road as seen by Bishop de la Mota y Escobar in the first decade of the seventeenth century reveals the route along the Camino Real northward from Guanajuato toward Zacatecas. That line continued northward as silver was discovered in the outreaches of land belonging to the Tarahumara and their allies along the Camino Real, which was the supply line for the missions in their midst on the slopes of the Sierra Madre Occidental. The widest east–west extension of his pastoral *visita* presented a panoramic vista to a frontier stretching from the west coast of Sinaloa eastward to Nuevo León near the Gulf of Mexico. The long south-to-north extension of his travels ran from Colima to Nueva Vizcaya, present-day Chihuahua.[24]

Bishop de la Mota y Escobar recounted the early days of Jesuit missionaries in Nueva Galicia (Nueva Vizcaya). By 1600, the missionary field had expanded to the lands of the Tepehuan and the Tarahumara. Quietly, Father Juan Fonte, a Jesuit, had taken the long trip along the Camino Real to the mining frontier in Durango. Before long, by 1610, he had established a small mission at present-day Balleza, then called San Pablo.[25] Fonte was able to reconcile two tribes, the Tepehuan and the Tarahumara, and moved a contingent of them to a small mission site near present-day Santa Bárbara in Chihuahua. His success was short lived as he and another missionary were killed in the first attacks of the Tepehuan uprising in 1616. In the rebellion, "two hundred Spaniards were sacrificed including ten friars. Of the ten priests killed by the Tepehuanes, only four bodies were recovered. An estimated thousand Tepehuanes were killed. Mines, roads, and ranches were ruined."[26] Within a short time, Christianized Tepehuan and Spanish settlers returned and restored their settlements. Meanwhile, many tribes joined the Tepehuan and Tarahumara as they withdrew into many of the high mountains, ravines, and canyons in the Sierra Madre.[27]

In his eyewitness account, Bishop de la Mota y Escobar gave information about towns, their founding, and their purpose. Everywhere Bishop de la Mota y Escobar went, he noted which towns had mills, which had cattle, which had mines, which had stores, and which religious orders ministered sacraments to frontiersmen in peril of losing their souls. His descriptions of small villages or settlements; his scrupulously kept statistics about people and animals; and his observations about the land, mines, mills, commerce, ethnography, and politics along the route painted an extraordinary picture of the line of settlement along the Camino Real and other areas in Nueva Galicia.

He noted, for example, that Lagos was situated on the Camino Real that went from Mexico City to Zacatecas, one of the most traveled roads of the period. Lagos, wrote Bishop de la Mota y Escobar, was established in 1561 as a defensive post against Indians, but equally so, its location was chosen because of the fertility of the soil, which contributed to its agricultural potential. Bishop de la Mota y Escobar pointed out that firewood was scarce because Lagos was so far from the wooded mountains in the vicinity.[28] Cerro Gordo, a nearby mountain, was a haven for enemy Indian tribes, which included the Copuces, the Zacatecas, and the Guachichiles, who raided Spanish settlements, including Lagos. The structures at Lagos, he wrote, were architecturally more like towers and fortifications than well-ordered residences. Lagos had twenty Spanish citizens, who appeared quite wealthy compared to others in the vicinity. A parish church was financed through tithing. Well situated along the Camino Real, Lagos was blessed by two rivers nearby that provided catfish and other fish. A large lake close to Lagos provided wildlife that supplemented the village diet.[29] On the Camino Real, Lagos was well supplied with all kinds of clothes, wine, vinegar, raisins, and almonds from Mexico and other provisions.[30] Bishop de la Mota y Escobar felt Lagos was one of the best situated towns in Nueva Galicia.[31]

In contrast, he saw the Villa de Aguascalientes when it was still a growing village with adobe houses badly laid out. In its midst was a parish church. Then, Aguascalientes was mostly inhabited by poor but rugged mestizo frontiersmen who herded cattle.[32] Aguascalientes, wrote Bishop de la Mota y Escobar, was so named "for some hot springs that are near there; a year-round arroyo runs past the houses from which all the neighbors drink, and although the water runs hot, it neither tastes like asufre, alumbre nor herrumbre [sulfur, alum, nor rust]; when it is chilled, the water is very sweet and salubrious."[33] The people were poor and served the large landowners by herding their large herds of varied livestock. At Aguascalientes, the people did not farm. When they did trade it was only for mares, horses, mules, and cattle.[34] Zacatecas was not far from there.

Regarding Zacatecas, Bishop de la Mota y Escobar not only revealed something about daily life in towns on the Camino Real; he also noted the historical process that was leading north to the lands of the Tarahumara and their allies. Bishop de la Mota y Escobar recorded how much development had taken place within Indian territorial lands. Rich in gold and silver, the hills around Zacatecas formed a fabulous treasure waiting to be excavated.[35] They were discovered in 1540 by Juan de Tolosa, a Basque.[36] La Bufa, a large hill, held rich deposits that made Zacatecas one of the wealthiest areas on the Camino Real. The common language among the settlers of Zacatecas was Spanish, but many Indigenous tongues were spoken owing to the presence of a sizeable population of "mexicanos, otomíes, tarascos and other nations."[37] Zacatecas was filled with various mechanics, tailors, carpenters, and smiths.[38] Among other resources in Zacatecas, he noted that firewood was expensive because settlers had denuded the vicinity of trees. Firewood was carted in on the large, solid-wheel carretas and sold at the highest price. The situation was similar at Lagos. In Zacatecas, Spaniards, mestizos, Indian laborers, and Black and mulatto slaves lived in many of the three hundred adobe houses, which were nothing more than hovels, with a few stone structures. He described four plazas that were connected by one main road. Franciscans, Jesuits, and Augustinians competed in Zacatecas, for there was only one parish church. Among his many observations, Bishop de la Mota y Escobar wrote about the history and politics of the mines in Zacatecas.[39]

At Fresnillo, for example, he saw twelve mills; at the Hacienda de Medina on the northern edge of the Zacatecas mining frontier, he headed toward Nueva Vizcaya (present-day Chihuahua), where he saw cultivated fields, livestock, and mills for processing silver.[40] Beyond there, at Pueblo de Sain, he saw livestock in the area and two water-run mills for processing ore, indications of an incipient economy based on mining.[41] At Sombrerete, which he called Real de Minas de Sombrerete, and Villa de Llerena, he wrote that the richest ores had already been extracted although five or six haciendas with their mills still in operation along with a Franciscan convent.[42] Just west of Sombrerete, Bishop de la Mota y Escobar found Real de Minas de San Martín, in mountainous terrain. He noted its economic decline as a mining area with five or six Spanish residents sustained by groves of apple trees, a product in demand among miners in the area.[43]

Traveling northward past Chalchihuites to Valle de Suchil, located between Sombrerete and Nombre de Dios in present-day Durango, Bishop de la Mota y Escobar was impressed with its fertility and its eight productive farms.[44] Beyond there, he veered west toward Nombre de Dios. Once there, de la Mota y Escobar described the town as hot and humid, with a stream that carried water year-round. Nombre de Dios, he wrote. had been founded to defend the road from Chichimeca raiders. At that time, Nombre de Dios was a *paraje*, or stopping place, on the Camino Real, situated on the northern edge of Nueva Galicia. At the time of his *visita*, Nombre de Dios had fifteen to twenty resident Spaniards living in small adobe houses who owned large farmlands nearby. Near there, fifty to seventy Indians lived in a small pueblo with a Franciscan convent.[45]

In the vicinity of Nombre de Dios, at Asiento del Capitán Lois, Bishop de la Mota y Escobar found four water-driven mills, some for processing ore and others for grinding wheat. He also observed livestock and an abundance of wildlife in the area. From there, he went to Real de Minas de las Nieves and saw much livestock, plentiful water, and large cultivated fields. There, he saw four or five mills for processing ore and a mule-driven mill.

West of there was the working Estancia del Comendador Rodrigo del Río with large numbers of enslaved people, Indian servants, and mulattoes who worked as herders and field hands.[46] Beyond Real de Joachín and San Juan de Mezquital, inhabited by one hundred Chichimecas, Bishop de la Mota y Escobar reached Gracián, which was known for its coal mines.[47]

On to La Punta by way of Valle de las Poanas, Bishop de la Mota y Escobar mentioned crossing a large stream called Los Berros.[48] From there, de la Mota y Escobar traveled to Tunal, a pueblo of peaceful Chichimeca farmers. A Franciscan priest attended to their spiritual needs.[49] At that point, de la Mota y Escobar had meandered in and around present-day Durango and, barely six miles from there, had turned southwest. Not far from Avino, de la Mota y Escobar passed through Peñol Blanco, a place with several mines and two water-driven mills.[50]

From there, Bishop de la Mota y Escobar, again changing directions, meandered to Cuencamé. Of the mines there, he wrote that they had been recently discovered, sometime in 1601. Most of the mines were on one mountain. A parish church had already been constructed there to serve more than a hundred Spanish residents. Franciscan missionaries worked among the Chichimecas, after whom the town was named.[51]

Beyond there, Bishop de la Mota y Escobar's next stop was in the Valle de San Bartolomé. There, he saw all kinds of crops and livestock owing to an irrigation system. Industrious frontiersmen had built mills for flour to sell to nearby miners. Wildlife abounded and de la Mota y Escobar reported seeing geese, ducks, and cranes at a marsh not far from the Spanish settlement. At that time, Franciscans from Santa Bárbara made weekly visitations to the parish church there.[52] Nearby, at Todos Santos, Bishop de la Mota y Escobar noted eight to ten Spaniards running a mule-driven mill there. Aside from an abundance of water and wildlife, they raised wheat and other crops as well as livestock for sustenance. De la Mota y Escobar wrote that Todos Santos was the last settlement in the northwestern part of Nueva Vizcaya. Beyond that point began the large expanse leading to New Mexico.[53]

By 1641, development of Spanish settlements, mines, and mission was under way. Caravans of supplies were brought up the Camino Real to supply the miners and settlers. Franciscan and Jesuit missionaries relied on the caravan to bring up not only supplies but also church ornaments and materials for the interior of the new churches they were building. They were supported by alms given by settlers to the church for such objects and materials as well as foodstuffs.[54] The use and extent of the Camino Real de Tierra Adentro that intertwined Indian pathways and Spanish routing developments to places far to the north like New Mexico formed a large part of the history and heritage of the area.

Were it not for the diligent eye of Alonso de Benavides, the Franciscan prelate and custodian of the Holy Office of the Inquisition in New Mexico in 1626, a panoramic view of the Camino Real in New Mexico beyond Nueva Vizcaya would be lacking. In his *Memorial of 1630* and his *Revised Memorial of 1634*, Benavides records invaluable descriptions of villages and people north of El Paso, which by now was the recognized gateway to New Mexico. Like Bishop de la Mota y Escobar, Benavides traveled the land and recorded his observations for his superiors to use in promoting the missionary field in "la conversión de San Pablo en la provincia de Nuevo México." Of the southern limit of New Mexico, Benavides, writing through Spanish colonial eyes, explains,

> The kingdom of the provinces of New Mexico are situated four hundred leagues beyond the City of Mexico, to the north at 37°. And, although the settlements are situated there, the district really begins two hundred leagues before that point, that is, in the Valley of Santa Bárbara, the last pueblo of New Spain in that direction. The dividing line is the Conchos River, so named because of the Concha nation which dwells there. From here we travel on for a distance of one hundred leagues in search of the Río del Norte, and we do this at very great risk, because the route passes through the territory inhabited by the Tobosos, Tarahumares, Tepioanes, Tomites, Sumas, Janos and other very ferocious, barbarous and indomitable tribes. . . . We have made every effort to convert and pacify these nations, both for the good of their souls and the safety of the road. . . . Having traversed these hundred leagues, we arrive at the famous Río del Norte.[55]

Beyond the ford of the Río del Norte, it appears that Benavides traveled through an area inhabited by the Apaches del Perrillo, which was present-day Jornada del Muerto. El Perrillo, the water hole named during the Oñate expedition of 1598 that found water in a seemingly waterless plain by following the tracks of a small dog, thus *perrillo*, had given way to a toponym as well to the designation of an Apache tribe, probably part of the Mescaleros or Mimbreños.[56] By the end of the seventeenth century, Nueva Vizcaya witnessed that the same route and land to the north described by Benavides had been consumed by the Pueblo Revolt of 1680.

Notably, sixty-four years before the Pueblo Revolt of 1680, the Tepehuan Revolt of 1616 began in Sinaloa south of Tarahumara country.

The relationship between the Pueblo Revolt and the Tepehuan Revolt points to the fact that some Native rebellions were associated with others elsewhere in northern New Spain such as New Mexico. Defense of homeland was a common theme engrained in causes for rebellions that were constant and pervasive throughout the Americas.

The Pueblo Revolt of 1680, a prelude to the Tarahumara rebellion of 1690, is part of the history of the Camino Real, for it resulted in an event in which Hispanic refugees, using the Royal Road, fled southward from Santa Fe past the pueblos of the lower Rio Grande to El Paso, where they remained until 1692, within range of the Tarahumara rebellion of 1690.

Spanish officials led sorties northward along the Camino Real through Nueva Vizcaya, to reconnoiter the damage done to the land they had occupied since 1598. The Tarahumara and their allies watched as Spanish troops moved northward. Some expeditions hoped to retake New Mexico sooner, but it was not until 1692 that the "Reconquest" began. That year, Diego de Vargas led an army northward along the Camino Real, past the lands of the Tarahumara and their allies, and succeeded in gaining a foothold in Santa Fe, which led to the recolonization of New Mexico. The Camino Real had witnessed a pageantry of settlers, soldiers, friars, fugitives, and refugees in colonial New Mexico's history. The Tarahumara and their allies knew well how the Pueblo Revolt of 1680 had succeeded and ended as the pageantry of war had passed through the middle of Nueva Vizcaya.

CHAPTER 4

A JESUIT'S VIEW FROM THE MONTAÑAS DE GUAZAPARES

Padre Neumann's 1724 Account of the Tarahumara Rebellion of 1690

On May 1, 1723, Father Joseph Neumann, sitting at a table at Mission Carichiqui, in the Tarahumara mission field, dipped his quill pen into a small cup of sepia ink and prepared a letter to the Padre Provincial de Bohemia. With it, Father Neumann submitted a copy of his manuscript titled "Historia de las Rebeliones de los Tarahumaras" with the expressed hope that he and the people of Bohemia would know about that part of the world. To that end, he dedicated his book to the missionaries past and present who had worked there during his tenure. Having served at the mountainous terrain at Guazapares for sixteen years, he knew the story well.[1] He also hoped to express his gratitude to his superiors who had appointed him to serve the Tarahumara. He began by saying that at age forty-three he was appointed to the province of Nueva Vizcaya in Mexico in 1678 by Father General Gian Paolo Oliva. Two years later, he arrived at the Tarahumara mission field. During his mission in Tarahumara country, he served as Father Superior of that mission field as well as having served as Father Visitor to the missions in the area at the request of missionaries working there.[2] Although factually accurate, Father Neumann's story was told the only way he knew how: as a member of the brotherhood of missionaries who saw the world through Spanish colonial eyes.

Father Neumann began his account by stating that the Tarahumara occupied almost all of Nueva Vizcaya. Parral was the main Spanish settlement and was about two hundred leagues (actually nearly eight hundred miles) north of Mexico City. While silver was discovered around 1631, he wrote that the Spanish settlers had explored a wide region within Nueva Vizcaya, which appeared to be uninhabited for settlement purposes. Within that area, they had hoped to establish villages, farms, and ranch lands. They had tried to win over the Tarahumara with trade and friendly relationships. One of the first settlements in that area was a settlement called Villa de Aguilar, within the Valle de Papigochi, in 1649. There, settlers planted wheat fields and established pasturage areas for their animals.[3]

Soon after, not far from Villa de Aguilar, Father Corneille Beudin established a mission at Papigochi. There, along a riverbank, he set up a small chapel to say the Holy Mass. Aside from giving them small gifts in friendship, a large part of his time was spent trying to instruct the Tarahumara abut Christianity. Similarly, his comrade Father Giácomo Basile established a mission at Teméichi, about twenty-six miles away. Despite their efforts, the Natives were very much irritated by the presence of the settlers at Villa de Aguilar and the nearby mission within their lands.

From the early days of the missionary efforts that had been undertaken as early as 1604, resentment among the Tarahumara and their allies brewed in the background. For example, the early phases of missionization of the Tarahumara and Tepehuan were interrupted by the Tepehuan Revolt of 1616. By 1639, Jesuit missions among the Tarahumara and Tepehuan were established between Durango and Chihuahua at Balleza, San Felipe, San Jerónimo Huejotítlan, San Pablo de Tepehuanes, and San Javier de Satebó.[4] Resentment among the Tarahumara and other allies did not go away. All were unhappy with the Spanish missions and settlements on their land. Their unhappiness was not only expressed in the occupation of their lands by settlers, miners, and missionaries; they despised the idea that their beliefs and their spirit world were at odds with Christianity. It was repeatedly clear, on the other hand, as seen by missionaries, settlers, and soldiers in the area, that the Tarahumara and their allies did not want them on their land.[5] In the late 1640s, signs of a rebellion could be felt with a series of small attacks against settlers and presidial soldiers.

Throughout each uprising, Spanish settlers and missionaries identified the leaders who swore to expel them from their land. Vociferous and daring, Tepehuan and Tarahumara leaders from time to time rose to the occasion to drive out the Spaniards and their Indian allies. Leading the Tepehuan warriors in the 1616 uprising, for example, was Quautlatas, an *hechicero*, once a baptized Christian, who predicted that the Spaniards would be driven out and the Tepehuan would dominate their land. That rebellion succeeded for a short period of time, as Spanish settlers and miners did not return to Papasquiaro, Santa Catalina, Zape, and other places in that area until 1623.[6]

Strong anti-Spanish sentiments among the Tepehuan and Tarahumara lingered into the next decade. In 1632, for example, Father Neumann mentioned another uprising in out-of-the-way Chínipas. There, as he described him, Cobamea, a famous but fierce and cruel leader, rose up against the Jesuit missionaries, Spanish miners, and settlers. His main goal was to rid the area of all Spaniards, missionaries, settlers, and miners alike. To him, rebellion was the only way for the people of Chínipas to recover their freedom.[7] Cobamea's rebellion spread to Guazapares, Témoris, and other nearby settlements, with devastating effects. Indeed, the Spaniards and missionaries were caught off guard as they were celebrating the feast day of San Ignacio de Loyola. Cobamea's rebellion was successful in driving out miners, settlers, and missionaries from the area who abandoned their missions and mines for nearly three decades.[8]

In his recollection of another rebellion, Father Neumann describes the initial shock of the rebellion that took place in the early days of June 1650. Of it, he writes:

> The natives met and were in agreement and hatched a conspiracy. They called out to all Indians of their nations, no matter how far away. They set the month and day and finally, as they had ordered previously, they all gathered in a certain place in the *valle*—well armed with bows and quivers filled with poisoned arrows, slings and wooden lances—among the weapons they use. All ready to march, with loud shouts and tumult in mind, they attacked the first place—that of Padre Corneille, who was at his home in Papigochi. There, the Tarahumares surrounded him, as he embraced the *cruz* [cross] that was on his front door—and clubbed him with their *macanas* [wooden weapons] and shot him with arrows.[9]

Having burned down the church and desecrated the sacramental ornaments, they proceeded against the mission at Teméichi, where they killed Father Giácomo Basile.

There, some forty years later, after the next major rebellion of 1690, Teméichi was revisited. On the site of the rebellions, among the debris of the church, settlers found the remains of Father Basile—"his skull, and skeleton—and his Jesuit cassock wrapped around his neck."[10] To them, it marked the spot where he was killed. His remains and other church artifacts were moved to a vault at the reconstructed church at Papigochi sometime after 1690.[11]

The rebellion of 1650 was fast and furious. Spanish soldiers pursued them through the mountains until they surrendered. They did so because they were out of food and were desperately hungry. Within a few months, the Tarahumara and their allies returned to their old homes and the Spaniards to Parral or to their villages. Once back, they resumed working the silver mines. It appeared, as Father Neumann recounted, that peace was at hand in the region around Papigochi.[12] Still, the next thirty years saw outbursts among the Tarahumara and their allies against Spanish occupation of their lands.

By 1680, six new missionaries joined the lone missionary, Tomás Guadalajara, in the Tarahumara mission field. They were Nicolás Ferrer, assigned to Papigochi; José Sánchez de Guevara went to Teméchi y San Bernabé; Antonio de Oreña served at Sisoguíchi; Francisco de Arteaga went to Nonoaba and Humarisa; Diego Ruiz de Contraras went to Caricha; and Francisco de Celada served at San Francisco de Borja.[13] Of the six missionaries, three—Oreña, Ruiz de Contreras, and Sánchez—died of natural causes between 1684 and 1686.[14] In all, only four missionaries attended to the Tarahumara mission field before the 1690 rebellion.

The lonely missionaries worked throughout the vast Tarahumara land in all directions possible. Hopelessly, they considered that "it would be impossible to lead them to a Christian life unless we are able to congregate them into small pueblos."[15] Although different governors had tried to assist the missionaries in this effort, over time, without sufficient soldiers to do so, it was not successful. Indeed, between 1670 and 1690, attacks against travelers, settlers, miners, soldiers, and missionaries were carried out by the Tarahumara, Conchos, Chizos, Sumas, Mansos, Tanos, Tobosos, Julimes, and Opatas.[16]

Given the shortage of missionaries in the Tarahumara mission field as early as 1677, alarmed authorities petitioned Church officials in Mexico City to send delegates to Rome and Spain to inform authorities of the serious danger to the few missionaries in Nueva Vizcaya. In 1678, twenty-five missionaries, among them Father Neumann, were recruited and assigned to Tarahumara country. Given travel difficulties caused by a myriad of issues, including inclement weather, the recruited missionaries made their way by land across Europe to Cadiz in Spain and, from there, they made the difficult transatlantic voyage to Cuba. They reached Mexico in the fall of 1680 and were quickly sent north to Nueva Vizcaya.[17] Early snowfalls in the Sierra Madres added to the difficulty they endured as they made their way to the far reaches of the Tarahumara mission field. Having spent nearly two decades in the mountainous terrain at Guazapares, Father Neumann knew well the territorial limits of the Tarahumara mission field.[18]

From the very beginning of the conversion of the Tarahumara and their allies, rebellions were prevalent, and from time to time, signs of a possible rebellion flitted across the land. Indian raids throughout the area happened, such as in 1689 when settlements were hit and horses, cattle, and sheep were stolen. Soon, other warnings of the coming rebellion were at hand. Suddenly, in spring 1690, a new hard-hitting rebellion occurred when the mission at Yepómera, in the northern part of Tarahumara country, was attacked. According to Father Neumann, it was there, in the early morning, that Father Diego Ortíz de Foronda was killed, along with two others. The raiders ransacked the mission and took church ornaments and religious items belonging to Padre Foronda as well as livestock in the mission corrals.[19]

Father Francisco de Selada added information about what had occurred that day. It appeared that Father Foronda and his escort were waiting for other settlers who had been called back to aid their Indian allies, from Papigochi and Santo Tomas, when the violence originally hit. On their way to Yepómera, those settlers learned of the violence and deaths of the priest and his escorts. They were too late to help them.[20] They next went to Matachic, where certain missionaries had gone to celebrate Holy Week, prior to Easter commemorations, where they learned that the rebels were set to attack the mission pueblos between Yepómera and Sisoguíchi. The rebels, who had hit Yepómera, burned the church and other structures before leaving the area. It was noted that the Tarahumara, who lived in the area and had witnessed the violence, feigned ignorance and fear, giving the rebels free passage through the area.[21] Father Selada quickly communicated the event as he had heard the details from witnesses and remarked that once the rebels had retreated, the land was too rough and the distances between places were too far apart for any containment of the rebellion. He had also learned that the *naciones* in Ostumuri and the land of the Pima were also primed for rebellion. He had also heard that the tribes in the Valle de Papigochi had armed themselves in preparation for the rebellion. To make things worse, furthermore, the settlers in those areas were unprepared and cut off from any immediate assistance.[22]

In the wide-open and faraway reaches of the Tarahumara mission field, within the Valle de Papigochi and the surrounding area, another attack unfolded that foretold the extent of the rebellion. Father Neumann explained that the warring Indians came from four mission areas in the Sierra Madre Occidental: Yepómera, Temósachi, Nahuérachi, and Seirupa. They were influenced to attack by the Jovas, a neighboring mountain tribe.[23]

Quickly, missions at Cajurichi, Tomochi, Tatiana, Matachi, Cocomórachi, and Yepómera were attacked. As the rebellion spread, settlers at Cusihuiríachi abandoned their settlements and mines that had been recently established. Troops were deployed under General Juan Fernández de Retana, who, with fifty soldiers from Sonora, arrived at Papigochi. There, they awaited reinforcements made up of soldiers and Indian allies. Soon, Retana and his soldiers at Papigochi were attacked by a large rebel force.[24]

Father Neumann commented that the attackers were emboldened by an outspoken Indian leader who promised his followers that they ought not fear the Spanish arquebuses for they were incapable of firing, nor should they fear the musket balls. He exhorted the rebels, in messianic terms that had resounded from the Tepehuan Revolt of 1616, by assuring them that those killed by a Spanish lance or sword would rise again on the third day. With that, the Indians mounted a furiously violent attack against Retana's soldiers.[25]

Just moments before the attack, one of Retana's soldiers spotted a large movement of Indians moving in his direction. Quickly, he sounded the alarm and Retana's soldiers responded and formed a fire line. As the attackers ran toward them, they opened fire, killing and wounding many of them; in the melee, the Indian leader who had promised that the dead would rise again was himself killed. Before retreating, the warriors responded by shooting poisoned arrows at the Spaniards. The soldiers pursued them with their swords and lances. Having suffered some casualties, the warriors fled to the mountains whence they came.[26]

Meanwhile, having left Parral on June 12, 1690, Governor Juan Isidro de Pardíñas arrived in Papigochi, not long after the battle fought by Retana and his men, with two hundred armed reinforcements, which included a number of Indian allies. While en route, by way of Yepómera, the governor and his troops hoped to engage the retreating warriors but saw no sign of them.[27] They remained in Papigochi for a short while, hoping to determine the cause of the outbreak of violence. During that time, they explored the mountain terrain and found small groups of rebel Indians and captured them.[28] Throughout the campaign, Retana and his men made several sorties against the rebels and at one point reached as far east as the Río Conchos.

Neumann noted that in his investigation of the outbreak, Pardíñas discovered that there had been a conspiracy among eleven tribes for four years. Their aim was to rid the area of missionaries and Spanish settlers. During that four-year period, they waited for a good time to attack on a widespread basis. Pardíñas concluded that the uprising was a joint effort by the Tarahumara, Conchos, Sumas, Janos, Jovas, Julimes, Chinarras, Tobosos, Acoclames, Chizos, and Apache.[29] Those tribes were spread within a huge area of Nueva Vizcaya.

Hoping not to escalate the violence or encourage another uprising, Pardíñas decided to meet with the Tarahumara and seek peace. He released his prisoners and sent them as messengers several times to seek the Tarahumara to arrange a meeting.[30] But the Tarahumara refused to meet with him as they did not trust the Spaniards. Finally, after several attempts to communicate with them, they accepted the proposition that they would obey and put down their arms. To test their response, Pardíñas moved his troops from Papigochi to Carichí, about ten miles from Cusihuiríachi, a Jesuit mission.[31] It seemed peace had taken a new turn.

Meanwhile, the history of the Tarahumara rebellion soon took on a more sinister twist. A flurry of complaints against Governor Pardíñas's handling of the rebellion reached Mexico City. At first, he thought that it was the settlers at Parral who had sent various messages to the viceroy in which they accused him of having been the indirect cause for the rebellion. According to Father Neumann's history, the settlers felt that the governor had troubled the Tarahumara with his avaricious behavior.[32] In his account, Father Neumann did not specify any details.

As the people who sent the letters were not identified, Pardíñas concluded that it was the Jesuits who had sent the letters to the viceroy. In that case, he asked his officers to investigate and document that it was the Jesuits who had caused the rebellion. To that end, Pardíñas directed all blame for the rebellion to the Jesuits. The governor ordered that all messages sent south to Mexico City by the Jesuits be intercepted and collected.

Hoping to defend and exculpate the Jesuits, the Padre Visitador of the missions in Nueva Vizcaya decided to send Father Neumann to Mexico City to speak to the Padre Provincial and defend the Jesuits against such accusations. Neumann, at the mission of Sisoguíchi among the Tarahumara, traveled southwest from the mountains of Guazapares toward Sinaloa, a roundabout way to Mexico City, to avoid detection by Pardíñas's men.[33] Once there, Father Neumann not only met with the Padre Provincial but also had an audience with the viceroy, Conde de Galve, who admired the Jesuits for their work.

In Neumann's meeting with the viceroy, which lasted three hours, the discussion clarified where Spanish officials in Mexico City stood. The viceroy, for example, noted that he had seen the letters, some of which blamed Governor Pardíñas, and others praised him for the efforts he made to quell the rebellion. The viceroy did comment that both groups of letters were confusing; within the next six weeks, he sent communiques to Pardíñas to account for the recent outbreaks at the Jesuit missions and report on the causes and effects of the Tarahumara rebellion, which within that period had exploded into a full-fledged uprising.[34]

To clarify the Jesuit position, Father Neumann explained that he and his superiors were open to the viceroy's response and that he had come to Mexico City without any prohibition about what he could say in his discussions with those concerned. Thus, the origins of Governor Pardíñas's correspondence with Viceroy Conde de Galve were the result of both the need to clarify issues raised by the letters and for Pardíñas to submit his reports on the causes and effects of the Tarahumara rebellion. In effect, the viceroy clarified that the letters blaming the Jesuits were null and void—"todas quedaban sin efecto" (all were without effect).[35] Having spent six weeks in Mexico City consulting with Church and civil authorities, Father Neumann had succeeded in exculpating the Jesuits.

To remedy the situation, the viceroy corresponded with Pardíñas on matters related to the safety of the missions in Nueva Vizcaya. On December 24, 1690, for example, the viceroy ordered Pardíñas to keep track of all expenses dealing with the pacification and defense of the missions in the area of the Tarahumara rebellion. Given the complaints against the governor by the Jesuits, the viceroy ordered him to leave a guard of between twenty-five and thirty men at each mission to guarantee the safety of the missionaries. On January 3, 1691, the viceroy told Pardíñas that, for the safety of the missions within the pueblos, he was to allow the missionaries to participate in the election process of all Indian governors. The role of the Jesuits in that regard was necessary to allow missionaries and military officials to have a clear distinction between obedient Indians and the "unrested and wild" Indian foes. To avoid any local confrontations in which friendly Natives felt exploited, they were to be excluded from any work or service in the mines. On another matter, to assure the safety of the missionaries, in his letter of October 22, 1692, the viceroy ordered General Retana to visit the missions once a year to assure that peace was being maintained.[36]

CHAPTER 5

BETWEEN PEACE AND WAR

Governor Pardíñas and Tarahumara Country

Sitting at his desk in 1688, a year before the start of a major Tarahumara offensive, Juan Isidro Pardíñas, governor and captain general of Nueva Vizcaya, reflected on the current situation in the province and noted that the area was relatively peaceful. In his report of 1688 to the Spanish Crown, Governor Pardíñas explains, in justifying terms related to Spain's sovereign claim to Nueva Vizcaya, that during the first fifteen months of his governorship of the province, he had, as required, kept informed of the affairs throughout the area. He describes the province of Nueva Vizcaya as "a very fertile kingdom, for in it are grown all kinds of grain that are to be found in other parts of America." Cattle and sheep ranches had been established to support the miners who found gold and silver in a land that "is extremely rich in gold and silver ores, for there is no part in the whole of it that does not show veins."[1] The problem, Pardíñas notes, revolved around the difficulty to work in that land because of the fear of the tribes in the area that continually waged war against them. As a colonial official, Pardíñas did not fully comprehend the extent to which the Tarahumara and their allies resented the presence of the Spanish and their Nahua allies who occupied their lands.

Optimistically, however, he notes that the Tarahumara had been recently converted to Christianity, which had made it safer to seek gold and silver in certain areas of the land. Pardíñas adds that during that time, miners had begun working in those areas. He was hopeful that settlements could be firmly established throughout the province. He was less encouraged about the situation in the greater part of Nueva Vizcaya where Spaniards feared to tread. Mining and settlement efforts in many parts of the province were frustrated by constant violent attacks against Spanish settlers, miners, and missionaries.[2]

In his report, aside from settlements and mines in outlying areas and along the Camino Real, Pardíñas surmises that "the greater part of this kingdom has no Spanish population, for since the war in it has been continuous, the Spaniards do not venture to settle many parts that are very suitable for towns because of their lack of security against attacks by Indian enemies." Although he had carried out punitive attacks against them, he had not been able to pacify the area. He explains that "since this entire kingdom is such an open country, and the distance is very great across whatever section they invade in order to take horses and mules, [the situation had] frustrated the effort to mine for silver as no one can work there."[3]

No matter his thoughts about the violence in the province in 1688, early in the following year, 1690, officials witnessed a greater number of attacks against miners and settlers, a situation that broke out into a large-scale uprising of the Tarahumara that lasted nearly two years. Although Spanish soldiers had responded to small initial Tarahumara attacks that took place in 1689, their reports resulted in Spanish official preparations for war. Tensions among Spanish settlers and miners prevailed in Nueva Vizcaya as the Tarahumara and their allies prepared for a large-scale rebellion.

In 1690, just before the outbreak of the major offensive of the Tarahumara rebellion, Captain Francisco Ramírez, governor of Casas Grandes, sent a quick message to Governor Pardíñas and another notice of the same to Captain Juan Fernández de la Fuente, describing what he had seen and what information he could gather about the sudden attack in the areas around him. Namiquipa; the mines of Coyachi, Las Cruces, and La Boca de Candoga; and other places, he said, were no exception. There, pueblo leaders feared that one who inflamed the rebellion in consort with others, a "tlatole" who had led the attacks, would come back and kill them. He said that the Conchos had fiercely attacked places throughout the area near him and that the Natives who did not participate in the attacks were fearful and suspicious of anyone.[4]

At first, it appeared difficult to ascertain which individuals or tribes were involved in the uprising. For example, don Felipe, governor of Namiquipa, visited the Pueblo de San Miguel, which was believed to have been involved and that he had openly pronounced in favor of the uprising. When an attempt was made to arrest him, he fled to the mountains. He was tracked down and killed in a gunfight.[5] There were other incidents that preceded the rebellion.

As early as February 1690, Father Foronda, a month before his death, had noticed strange activities near Yepómera. He wondered about the movements made by certain tribesmen among the Jovas, Janos, Conchos, and Chinarras. It seemed they were killing horses and mules and gathering meat from the dead animals for future supply use. In a series of days, he had received notice from informants that aside from movement of groups of people, they had been seen rounding up other horses and mules. Such activity, to Father Foronda, seemed unusual. It appeared to him that they were up to some mischief. The Indians told him, however, that they had eaten the horse meat because they were hungry and that they were not as vile or wicked as they may have appeared to him.[6] Nonetheless, to Father Foronda, their behavior seemed to have been warning signs of what would be coming.

Father Foronda was not alone in his observations as a number of reports came in from various military observers at Jesús de Bacanuche, Nuestra Señora de Rosario de Nacosari, and the Presidio de San Phelipe y Santiago de Janos reporting similar activities and warnings of a possible large-scale uprising.[7] Apparently, Ramírez had communicated with Captain Juan de Escalante, telling him of the fast emerging need to be ready as the Conchos and other nations have united with the Tepeguanes, Chinatas, and Guazpares along with Pimas. Additionally, many of the Christianized Indians had fled to the mountains. Similarly, he had received a letter from Father Francisco de Velasco asking for military aid. Under those circumstances, Juan de Escalante ordered some soldiers that he had left at Baveachi to go and assist Ramírez and Father Velasco. It appeared to Escalante that the threatened area stretched from Namiquipa to points along the Sonora–Chihuahua mountains and valleys.[8]

On March 10, fearing an uprising, Captain Francisco Ramírez wrote to the governor saying that he had noted that the military post under Captain Fernández de la Fuente in Sonora had a weak force that needed arms, musket balls, and powder. Ramírez had noted that warriors from Sinaloa had infiltrated the area and the bordering Sonora and that one Indian had presented him with an arrow saying he had been sent by the Conchos. Realizing the symbolism of the arrow, Ramírez beseeched the governor to send soldiers to help in case they were needed quickly to defend the area.[9] Given the slowness of communication, on March 20 Ramírez noted the delay in the governor's response and on March 21 indicated that he would accept whatever assistance the governor could give.[10]

During that time, Governor Pardíñas had been busy consulting and evaluating the situation based on other reports from other military posts that the Yaquis, Sinaloas, Conchos, and other nations had formed a confederation and were readying their warriors for a rebellion. To that end, he had ordered soldiers to be ready to help, rescue, and provide defenses in those cases. He furthermore realized that other posts in the area were without sufficient arms and power to provide an adequate defense. He ordered General Fernández de Castañeda at the Real y Mines de Cosiguriachi to meet with settlers and miners in the area to prepare their defenses in case of attack.

On March 25, he called his generals to meet in a council of war.[11] Among those who met were generals Joseph de Neira, Juan Hurtado de Castilla, Juan Cortes del Rey, Captain Diego de Maturana, Sargento Mayor Agustin Herbante Camino, and others.[12] That day, he dispatched Captain Fernández de la Fuente to Casas Grandes to prepare for when the threatening uprising would take place. He also ordered Captain Juan Fernández de Retana from the Presidio de San Francisco de Conchos to go to San Pedro de Conchos and for General Marcos Fernández de Castañeda at Coyachic to send Francisco de Ramírez the needed gunpowder. Furthermore, Fernández de Castañeda was to prepare for the threatened uprising.[13] Five days later, they received notice of the uprising at Yepómera, where Father Foronda and his escorts were killed. They also learned of widespread destruction of missions and their churches, mines, settlements, and military posts.

At that point, the die was cast. Reports from most of Nueva Vizcaya in the Valle de Papigochi were of widespread destruction. Words flitted around that all the Indians of the Pueblo de Namiquipa had fled to the mountains, leaving those who did not flee without manpower for defense purposes. General Fernández de Castañeda noted that he had sent Captain Francisco de Archuleta into the area to organize whatever defenses could be made. He confirmed that most at Namiquipa had fled. Lacking the proper manpower for defense of the area, he asked the governor for fifty men to provide a defense before all would be lost. To best provide for supplies and food, they would be needed to round up cattle by day, for nighttime was too dangerous to be outdoors.[14] Other areas in the Valle de Papigochi underwent the ravages of war as missionaries, settlers, miners, military personnel, Christian Indians, and allied tribes all suffered. In its outbreak, the Tarahumara rebellion of 1690–93 had made its point in terms of defense of homeland, but, as it turned out, they were unable to drive the Spanish usurpers from their land.

For the next few years, Nueva Vizcaya witnessed several outbreaks as the rebellion continued to flare in various locations. Finally, in 1693, after the Tarahumara rebellion of 1690 had been suppressed, Governor Pardíñas, as required by the viceroy, investigated the causes of what they called the "uprising of the Tarahumaras and their allies in Nueva Vizcaya." In his reports, Governor Pardíñas affirmed that the Tarahumara rebellion had been put down and that the Tarahumara and their allies had peacefully settled in their pueblos. He assured that the Jesuit and Franciscan missionaries could return to their missions.[15]

As an incentive, the viceroy provided funds for the missions to purchase new ornaments for the altars and assured missionaries that it was safe to pray the Holy Mass on the sites of the destroyed churches. The viceroy also ordered Pardíñas to provide for the safety of the missionaries by assigning twelve soldiers to each mission for their protection. The viceroy also ordered that the soldiers remain at the mission sites until the churches had been restored.[16] Moreover, the viceroy ordered that the Tarahumara missions be protected by an escort guard (*escolta*) comprising thirty soldiers so that the missionaries could travel to and from each mission.[17]

Governor Pardíñas demurred from such an order, arguing that he had two hundred soldiers divided into four units at the ready to launch an attack if needed and there was no need for an *escolta* for the missionaries. In other words, should there be another uprising, the soldiers stationed at the mines of Cusihuiríachi were on alert in case of trouble. It appeared that the Jesuits quietly accepted the governor's noncompliance to the viceroy's order and, especially after fleeing the attacks in 1690, wisely did not return to their missions until 1692 or later.[18] It appeared that throughout the Spanish colonial period, governors and officials often did not comply with their superior's orders by privately whispering the words, "obedezco pero no cumplo" (I obey but do not comply).

A military meeting at the onset of the rebellion, referred to as the Junta de Capitanes, revealed some of the activities taken by Pardíñas and his officers. Regarding the referenced Junta, Pardíñas noted and reported its business on April 3, 1690. The purpose of the meeting was to strengthen defenses against the rebel uprising and report all actions taken to that end. Captain Antonio de Medina, for example, had taken twenty soldiers to reconnoiter an area within the Valle de Papigochi around Cosiguriachi. He was joined by General Marcos Fernández de Castañeda with twenty soldiers and Indian allies in the Valle de Papigochi who reported to him about friendly pueblos in the area. Meanwhile. General Juan Fernández de Retana marched from the Sonora side of the mountains to the Valle de Papigochi with twenty-five soldiers. While scouting the area, the officers of each unit stationed small contingents of soldiers to protect certain positions near friendly Indian pueblos.[19] In his report to the viceroy, Pardíñas referred to that and other reports he had gathered.

In 1693, Spanish officials, reviewing all reports and correspondence related to Native uprisings in Nueva Vizcaya, sought to determine the causes and effects of Indian rebellions, particularly that of the Tarahumara. While rebellions had taken place in Nueva Vizcaya throughout the seventeenth century, Spanish officials seemed perplexed regarding the outbreak of a major rebellion that nearly drove Spanish settlers out of the province.

Taking testimonies from Spanish participants between 1693 and 1695, Pardíñas explained the causes, both immediate and long-standing, and remedies that resulted in policies to bring the warring tribes into a mission system for pacification purposes. In his letter to the viceroy, Governor Pardíñas presented an account of six testimonies related to the uprising of the Tarahumara and their allies.[20] Yet their reasoning regarding causes, as evident in Pardíñas's earlier report of 1688, reflected a colonial viewpoint.

The first account, titled "Nueva Vizcaya año 1693" by Governor Pardíñas, explained the efforts made to pacify the Tarahumara and their allies, "Pibas, Tobas, Conchos, and Tepeguanes."[21] The second testimonio was made by General Juan Fernández de Retana, who had carried out Governor Pardíñas's orders to put down the rebellion. Additionally, as instructed by the viceroy, Retana continued to visit each pueblo annually to check on their pacificism.[22] Similarly, Captain Francisco Ramírez and Captain Juan Fernández de la Fuente, both of whom attended to the rebellion led by the Conchos in its early stages, explained the situation they faced.[23]

As Ramírez and Fernández attended to the uprising of the Conchos in and east of the Sierra de Tarahumares, they submitted their account of what they witnessed. Having patrolled from the Sonora side of the mountain to Namiquipa, they noted the poverty in the area among Spanish settlers who did not even have money to buy gunpowder or musket shot. Fernández de la Fuente noted the lack of soldiers in the area, as in one area he reported that there were two settlers and a priest and in another only four settlers, who told him they were virtually defenseless. They traversed a large area east from Namiquipa and met two Indians from Casas Grandes who said that the pueblos in the area did not admit any Conchos in their villages. Most Indians in the area they met were peaceful and the governors of the pueblos did not want to meet in any council or with a council representative (*tlatole*) because they feared meeting and discussing anything having to do with the uprising; they also feared they would be the first ones killed as informants. Before returning to Sonora, Fernández de la Fuente moved the settlers to nearby Spanish settlements.[24]

Pardíñas's preliminary report of April 20, 1690, written in the early days of the rebellion, offered a military account that supported Father Neumann's account written in 1724. In his account, following the outbreak of a major rebellion, Governor Pardíñas explained that the Tarahumara uprising had caused a great deal of damage and suffering throughout Nueva Vizcaya. Not only had the Tarahumara and their allies, particularly the Tepehuan and Conchos, killed missionary priests throughout the province; they had also destroyed and burned all the churches and mines, along with their equipment, as well as their adjoining settlements and military garrisons. The province lay in ruins.[25]

Given the situation, Pardíñas ordered punitive expeditions throughout the area to punish, subdue, bring the tribes back into the mission system, and pacify them throughout Nueva Vizcaya. Given the large expanse of the province, which included tribes in the difficult terrain of the Sierra Madre Occidental, Pardíñas explained that the initial military response began with the small number of soldiers within the province. Violent attacks, such as those at Bachimba, where lives were lost and buildings as well as mines were burned and destroyed, took place throughout the province. Meanwhile, the viceroy of Mexico ordered Pardíñas to investigate further into the causes for the uprising.[26]

Governor Pardíñas realized that the uprising was so widespread that it would take time and more soldiers to put it down. To that end, he explained to the viceroy that more soldiers and munitions were needed to complete this effort. He pointed out that the almost invincible warriors were so blatant that they attacked heavily fortified garrisons, like that at Bachimba, whose defenders, for the most part, were armed with arquebuses, which provided great firepower.[27] Throughout the province, particularly in the sierras where the terrain and the strong river currents impeded their movements, soldiers and settlers suffered small wounds and died days later because the warring tribes used poisoned arrows.[28] Pardíñas further noted that a major problem in the deployment of mounted troops in certain areas of the province was that the terrain was very difficult for horses or mules to maneuver and basically only foot soldiers could cross certain areas.[29]

In another instance, Pardíñas explained to Viceroy Conde de Galve that he and settlers throughout the province had continued to punish rebels wherever they could be located. He recounted an example where soldiers had pursued raiders to an unknown place, within the Valle de Papigochi, nearly seventy leagues (more than 180 miles from Parral) away, to a stronghold in the Sierra Madre. In one instance, they noted that the enemy they sought were not Tarahumara, even though their language was similar. They described the enemy as having the same appearance as Tarahumara but that their hairstyle differed. They said the young and adult warriors wore their hair similar to Ethiopians, a style they had not seen in other tribes in the area.[30] Not only were certain parts of the province unknown to them; so, too, were the numerous and differing tribes unfamiliar to them.

As a result of continuous warring, the need for more troops became a priority in putting down the uprising. In order to continue to suppress the rebellion, Pardíñas stressed the importance for more soldiers, ally warriors, and arms to reinforce the depleting number of troops on the ground in the province. Given the widespread violent and sudden uprising, many soldiers and their allies as well as the missionaries, caught by surprise, were forced to retreat from certain areas in the province.[31]

In most cases, the difficulty in reaching certain areas resulted from the centralized method in which the Jesuits had built churches and living quarters, generally three leagues (seven or eight miles) from Indian villages dispersed in differing directions, throughout the Sierra Madres and other mountain areas, to better serve them.[32] In that situation, Pardíñas explained that not all Tarahumara were at war. There were some loyal Natives who warned the Spaniards about the tribes they were facing.[33]

Among other factors revolving around causes of the rebellion, Pardíñas reflected on earlier rebellions in the province after which pacification through the mission process had taken place. He noted that such a peace with the warring tribes was not sincere. He said that thirty-seven years had passed since Governor Diego Guajardo Fajardo had put down the rebellion of 1653 and that the Jesuits had maintained a peace through missionization. Meanwhile, the Jesuits asked that a presidio be established in the area. During that period, 1649–50, Governor Guajardo Fajardo had established a presidio within the valley of Río Papigochi near the Villa de Aguilar—on the edge of the Sierra Madre Occidental west of present-day Cuidad Chihuahua.[34] To the Tarahumara, the establishment of a fort and a Spanish settlement represented an incursion onto their lands. Pardíñas believed that the intrusive placement of a fort in the midst of Tarahumara lands was a major cause of the 1653 rebellion.

According to the report issued by the Fiscal del Consejo de Indias, an official prosecutor from the Council of the Indies, Seville, Spain, which incidentally supported Pardíñas's conclusions, one important precedent that explained the difficulty in reducing the Indians to pueblos had antecedents in 1653.[35] That event resulted when Governor Guajardo Fajardo, after putting down another rebellion in Nueva Vizcaya, authorized Indians to establish their villages wherever they wished. A damning example related to the 1690 rebellion, cited in the fiscal's report, was the presidio that Governor Guajardo Fajardo had established in the Tarahumara province; the presidio did not prevent other rebellions, but its presence in the area likely caused them. The establishment of such a presidio also incurred additional expenses. Guajardo Fajardo's presidio and policies, according to the fiscal, were eight times more expensive than Pardíñas's campaign and resolutions.[36] Even so, Guajardo Fajardo's intrusive presidio encouraged greater animosity against the Spaniards among local Indians. The issue surrounding Guajardo Fajardo's presidio location in the Valle de Papigochi was used to justify the decision taken by Governor Pardíñas, and supported by Viceroy Conde de Galve, to deny the Jesuits' petition to establish a presidio in the Tarahumara province.

Pardíñas's decision generated tension between him and the Jesuit missionaries. Other issues that caused friction between the civil and the religious authorities surrounded the Jesuits' request for the Indians to pay for the reconstruction of missions and churches and their demand for direct participation in the election of Indian governors. In the end, while denying passing the cost of restoration of mission churches to the tribes, Pardíñas did grant the Jesuits' demand for them to participate in the pueblo elections.[37]

The fiscal's report was used by Governor Pardíñas to justify his decision, which was supported by Conde de Galve, to deny the Jesuits' petition to establish another presidio in the Tarahumara province. In the end, the fiscal's report of 1695 indicated that without a costly presidio, the Pardíñas campaign was eight times less costly than that of Governor Guajardo Fajardo.[38] The Jesuit response had been negative and generated further tension between them and the governor of Nueva Vizcaya. The Jesuit proposal for a heavily armed presidial garrison would have resulted in furthering the Tarahumara resentment to any Spanish presence within their territory. Even so, the Tarahumara and their allies bided their time for revolt.

Despite the Jesuit hope that the presidio and garrison such as that established by Guajardo Fajardo would stabilize the area, Pardíñas concluded that the plan did not work because it created distrust between the tribes against the missionaries and settlers in the area. He wrote that the establishment of a presidio in their midst did not have "good consequences," for the tribes felt that the garrison in their midst was meant to force them into a mission circumstance as well as to enslave them. The presence of such a presidial garrison placed by Guajardo Fajardo had resulted in several uprisings in the area.[39]

In referring to the rebellion of 1653, during Guajardo Fajardo's governorship, Pardíñas concluded that the relationships between the Tarahumara and the missionaries were false (*relaciones apócrifas*) and that the Jesuits had bought into the contradiction in which they were living. The Jesuit response to Pardíñas's attitude and comments resulted in sending Father Neumann to Mexico City to clarify issues regarding the governor's claim that the Jesuits were the cause of the rebellion. Indeed, the Jesuits viewed Pardíñas's refusal to establish a presidio to protect them as a reflection of his negative attitude toward them. Yet, at that moment, things seemed peaceful while the tribes they lived with seethed with resentment.[40]

With all that had happened, Pardíñas must have looked back on that fateful day of May 30, 1690, in the early phases of the rebellion, when he wrote to his superiors that he had received notice from a Jesuit who had sent a trusted Indian messenger from Papigochi to deliver a note that, in early April, the Tarahumara of Naguerachi had killed Father Diego Foronda, their minister, and two other Spaniards, Teniente Juan de Urias from the garrison at Yepómera and a settler, Francisco Fondes. Naguerachi was a *visita* of the main mission at Yepómera.[41] It seemed that Father Foronda had gone to Naguerachi to say the Holy Mass with Urias and Fondes as escorts. Yet, as he would later learn, there was more to the story. Meanwhile, Pardíñas continued his investigation into the causes of the rebellion.

Even though a presidial garrison with twenty to thirty soldiers had been established and local Tarahumara had warned both missionaries and settlers to expect more attacks against them, Pardíñas knew that he had to put down the rebellion if the province of Nueva Vizcaya was to be secured. Only time would prove if its success would hold. In his correspondence with the viceroy, he reiterated that the Tarahumara uprising had "taken the lives of their missionaries and destroyed and burned the churches as well as mines and haciendas." To that end, he had called a council of war. In the "junta de capitanes," as he called it, he declared the need to make the warring groups surrender, as he had reported to the viceroy. He also noted that the missionaries had to do their job in strengthening the mission field to promote "fraternal love" without the force of arms—particularly in the most remote parts of Nueva Vizcaya.[42]

Still, despite Pardíñas's attitude toward them, the Jesuits continued to assuage the hard feelings by teaching brotherly love to the Natives. Everyone agreed that placing a presidio in that country would strengthen control of the area. The issue at hand was that while the Jesuits had missionized a certain group, it was known that there were four different groups within the Tarahumara nation. Of the four, only one group had been worked by the missionaries and the rest were considered unconverted. Therefore, establishing a garrisoned fortification in the area would reduce attacks against missionaries and settlers.[43]

After the Tarahumara rebellion has been quelled by Pardíñas in 1693, the Indians were living in missions and villages under obedience to the king. As a matter of policy, it was clear that more Indians, under the tutelage of additional missionaries, would be pacified in this way. Because of that policy, the Spaniards were instructed to, when possible, live near the Indian villages, in order to discover more mines in those areas, thus increasing silver production. It was hoped that these new policies would calm the situation in dealing with the Indians by "not letting them suffer any form of violence or oppression."[44]

Pardíñas's investigation also focused on the rebellion in the area of Papigochi and Bachimba. The two areas bore much suffering, death, and destruction of property throughout the rebellion. The fighting at Bachimba, about twenty-six miles from Papigochi, appeared less intense, while at Papigochi, soldiers, settlers, and missionaries suffered high casualties and the destruction of churches and homes.[45] Bachimba was a mission run by Franciscans, while Papigochi was a Jesuit mission.

Defense of the province relied on the deployment of troops in all areas, from Sonora to the Valle de Papicochi across a wide expanse eastward to Namiquipa, and southward in Chihuahua to the southeastern edge of Sinaloa, where various tribes such as the Yaqui, the Conchos, and others were involved in support of the rebellion. Still, some scouting reports, such as one submitted on March 30, 1690, by Joseph de Turrado and others, who had been in certain areas far to the north, indicated that Casas Grandes, for example, had been very quiet. Similarly, Captain Fernández de la Fuente remarked that it seemed somewhat quiet in other areas near there.[46]

By 1693, the Indians were living in missions and villages under obedience to the king. It was hoped that these new policies would calm the situation in dealing with the Indians.[47] Still, the Tarahumara and their allies bided their time, as they had before, to rise up in their efforts to drive out the Spaniards from their traditional lands.

CHAPTER 6

RETANA'S MILITARY *VISITAS* TO VILLAGES AND MISSIONS IN THE VALLE DE PAPIGOCHI IN 1691–1692

In January 1692, in accord with the viceroy's recommendations, Governor Pardíñas ordered General Juan Fernández de Retana to begin a series of investigations regarding the causes and effects of the Tarahumara rebellion at several villages in the Valle de Papigochi. As ordered, Retana reported on the situation at each village he visited between 1691 and 1693.[1] Overall, his purpose was to gather information regarding the status of the pacification of the area. In a series of accounts, Retana reported that the pacification of the area had been relatively successful in quelling the rebellion. Dutifully, he toured several villages and missions in the Valle de Papigochi before returning to Parral.

Retana and his men had been in the area for a few months before he had received his orders to carry out the *visitas*, or inspection tours, to determine the status of the rebellion. On December 20, 1692, while at the Pueblo de Yepache, he found the Indians at peace. From them, he learned of the death of Ignacio Osebac, known as one of the prime leaders or *tlatole* of the Tarahumara Rebellion of 1690. Reviewing a letter from Father Neumann, it was, oddly, Osebac who had informed him that Father Foronda had been killed. Other informants had said that Osebac had planned to carry out other attacks on Spanish missions and villages. Yet there was some doubt in Retana's mind about Osebac's death. He looked into the issue and learned that some Tepehuan from the Pueblo de Sisoguíchi had, indeed, said that Osebac was dead. They also said that Osebac was known to them as Ignaciote, a native of Cocomorache. Yet Retana had also heard from others that Osebac was still alive. He asked that those witnesses be brought before him for interrogation into the death of Osebac. To Retana, the confirmation of Osebac's death would remain unresolved until just before his military *visita* was completed.[2]

That day, Retana interrogated a converted "Indio gentil" named Pato and another don Nicolás Garcia, a native of Babonoigua, a Tarahumara ladino who spoke Spanish, Tarahumara, and Pima. Swearing in, they made the sign of the cross. Don Nicolás said that he was not present when Osebac was killed but he heard from many other Tarahumara and Pimas that a nephew of Governor don Joseph of Tutuaca was there and he assured everyone there that whoever said Osebac was still alive was lying.[3]

Next, fifty-year-old don Joseph, governor of Tutuaca, testified that he was a native of Maicoba and that he was a Pima. Once sworn in, he stated that it was a lie that Osebac was still alive. He stated that his nephew had stated he was dead and had been killed somewhere along the Río de Yepache. He added that if Osebac were still alive, he would know it.[4] Soon after don Joseph had testified, his interpreter Salvador stated that he had not been present when Osebac was killed, but days later he heard from some relatives that Governor don Joseph had announced that "Ygnaciote" was dead and that his head had been sent to Parral. Beyond that, Salvador had not heard anything else.[5]

The next day, December 21, 1691, the *capitán general* of the Pima Nation, don Pablo Jumari, was sworn in. Although he had heard to the contrary, if he had believed otherwise, he would have looked for him just to make sure. But such was not the case. Don Pablo Jumari noted that the *tlatoles* in the area were uneasy. He stated that he was aware that when Retana entered Sonora to look for Osebac, many of them had heard that Osebac, taking his wife and child, fled to the Río de Yepache along with five other people. There, at the confluence with another river, they left him and his family. One of them was Osebac's nephew. His nephew left him to talk to a nearby chieftain named don Simón of the pueblo called Cocomorachic. The nephew said that he told don Simón where Osebac and his family were located. Apparently, don Simón was aware that a certain gentile Indian had found Osebac and his family hiding along the river. But soon after, following an altercation with his uncle, the nephew had raised his club and killed Osebac. One of the five men, having severed Osebac's head with a knife, had it wrapped in a manta and the nephew took the head to don Simón as proof that he was indeed dead. From there he took Osebac's head to don Manuel in Parral.[6]

The investigation into Osebac's death would continue into the next few months as Retana wanted to be absolutely certain about his demise and that the leader of the uprising was dead. It appeared that the Tarahumara uprising had been quelled, but the next month would be one in which Retana and his men, as instructed by Governor Pardíñas, had to make sure that the unrest had settled and that peace was at hand.

Having received his orders from Governor Pardíñas to reconnoiter the area by making military *visitas* to pueblos in the Valle de Papigochi to determine that the uprising was over, Retana and his command of twenty-five soldiers began their assignment. Traveling toward the post and Pueblo de San Marcos de Pichachigui, on January 6, 1692, Retana proceeded to Teméichi, where he interrogated Indian governor Manuel and the alcalde Nicolás. There, the village was at peace with more than a hundred mission and non-mission Indians. He learned that in the past two years, during the absence of missionaries, there were three children who had been previously baptized, but the priests had asked that those children that had not yet been baptized be identified. He noted that forty adults there had been baptized by Father Florencio de Alderete.[7]

On January 8, Retana approached the adjoining military post near the Pueblo de San Marcos de Pichachigui. There, he noted that the Natives were peacefully living in their terraced homes and tending their cornfields. Near their thatched-roof homes was a Ramada, which about one hundred Christian Indians and gentiles used to celebrate the Holy Mass. To Retana it was obvious that the people there had acquiesced to the guardianship of the local missionary priests.[8] The mission served nearby *visitas* at the Puesto y Caña de Tajubachi, six leagues away. There, the Natives were also at peace and, in cooperation with the priests, had their children baptized. Additionally, Father Florencio de Alderete had baptized forty-three adults.[9]

Retana compared the writings of Father Joseph Neumann to what don Manuel had told him. Earlier, Neumann, Retana noted, had told how

Ignacio Osebac had described the death of Father Diego Ortíz de Foronda, who was killed, along with two others, at the mission at Yepómera, in the northern part of Tarahumara country. According to Osebac, they were killed in the early morning.[10]

Following up on Neumann's rendition of the event, Retana confirmed that Ignacio Osebac was a *tlatole* and a leader in the rebellion. Given his knowledge of the Provincia de Sonora, Retana queried an informant who erroneously told him that Osebac had been killed by the Pimas and that his head, as well as that of Nicolás el Tuerto, was shown to General don Gerónimo, a Tarahumara chieftain.[11] Retana wanted to know the names of other *tlatoles.* The informant said he knew nothing about that or anything else. Retana retorted by asking how he could not know anything else when it was he who told Father Neumann about the death of Father Foronda and that the Natives at Sisoguíchi had told him about Osebac and the attacks elsewhere. Still, don Gerónimo stuck to what he had said, saying that he knew only what others had told him—nothing else.

To Retana the writings of Father Joseph Neumann appeared different from what don Manuel had told him regarding his testimony. Retana did not like his response. Again, he questioned how don Gerónimo could say he knew nothing when Father Neumann had stated that Gerónimo had testified that he knew about the uprising. But the forty-five-year-old don Gerónimo insisted that knew nothing, nor had he heard anything beyond some testimony given by others on that subject.[12]

Still, Retana persisted on finding out more about the *tlatole* Ignacio Osebac and his death. Reading through Father Neumann's statement made by fifty-year-old informant don Nicolas, alcalde at Teméichi, Retana learned that don Nicolas, in referring to the people at the Puerto de Chuita, had stated that he had heard from them that Ignacio Osebac had been killed at the Puerto de Moris de Pimas, which was located on both sides of the boundary line dividing Chihuahua and Sonora, and that his head had been delivered to don Gerónimo.[13] Although don Nicolas confirmed the death of Osebac, he also stated that he had not heard of an uprising at Puerto de Moris de Pimas.[14]

From there, two days later, Retana traveled to Nuesta Señora de Popula de los Álamos and noted the peaceful attitude of eighty-nine families who lived in their terraced houses and tended their cornfields. Retana ordered that new houses be constructed and those houses in disrepair be attended to. He also warned that anyone daring to round up beasts of burden be punished.[15] Perhaps Retana thought that horses would be used by raiding warriors.

At Nuestra Señora de Popula de los Álamos, he met with Father Florencio de Alderete, who discussed the wary but peaceful nature of the area. He noted that very few Jesuit missionaries had, prior to 1692, refused to return to missionize the area until it was secured. Father Alderete and Father Francisco María Piccolo, who had worked with the Tarahumara, agreed to send, at Retana's request, more missionaries to the villages as soon as possible.[16]

Soon after, Retana and his men proceeded to the Pueblo de Jesús Carichiqui on the thirteenth day of the month. There, he met with their leader, Governor don Nicolas, who swore obedience on behalf of the pueblo. The well-kept thatched-roof pueblo had more than two hundred families, who farmed their fields. Retana asked them to construct similar-style housing for the post he founded there, which they agreed to do.[17]

Assigned to the Pueblo de Jesús de Carichiqui were three *visitas*. One was at Tajirachi, which had seventy-five families who tended their cornfields. Another was at Bacareache. The third *visita* was at Pasigoche, which had fifty families. The area was divided into *partidos* (districts) under the ministry of Father Alderete. The Partidos de Matachiqui included Yepómera, Cocomorache, Arisiachi, Caurichi, and Tutuaca. The Natives within those areas lived similarly to those at the three *visitas*: living in thatched-roof houses and tending to their cornfields. Of that large missionary field, the minister added that there was much conversion work to do within the head mission, the *visitas*, and the districts.[18] Again, Retana asked that more missionary priests be assigned to those areas and Father Alderete issued another certification to do so.

Having visited Carichiqui, Tarirachi, Papigoche, and Bacauriache during a six-day period, January 13–19, Retana reported that the Indians peacefully attended to their lives in those areas. Accompanied by the two missionary priests, Father Alderete and Father Piccolo, he made plans to visit other pueblos in the area.

Soon after, on January 19–23, Retana continued his required military scouting *visita* at San Ignacio de Coiache, where he met with Father Miguel Ortega. Of his *visita* to Coiache, Retana wrote that the people there numbered 150 families, well situated in their thatched-roof houses.

There were two *visitas* assigned to Coiachi, one at Cosiguriachi, which had seventy families, and the other at Naguerachi, which had fifty-eight families.[19] Still, he had reason for concern as he noted that at La Concepción, forty-three warriors in the area of Coiachi appeared recalcitrant and ordered them to attend Holy Mass.[20]

Continuing on to Santa Isabel in the last week of January, Retana surveyed attitudes demonstrated by Natives in that area. At San Bernardino, between January 25 and 27, 1692, he met with forty Indians; at Santa Cruz, with forty Natives; at San Lorenzo, with ninety-five families; and at Puesto de Las cuevas, he found sixty-five families living in peace.

Moving ever forward with his task, given him by Governor Pardíñas, Retana, in the last week of January, continued to survey the attitudes of the Natives at Santa Isabel on January 25, 1692 (sixty-five Indians); the mission *visitas* at San Bernardino (forty Indians) and Santa Cruz (forty Indians); San Lorenzo on January 26, 1692, where he counted ninety-five families; and Puesto de Las Cuevas on January 27, 1692, with sixty-five families. While in that area, Retana heard about an *hechicero*, named Francisco, who had reportedly killed three Indians using witchcraft. It was said that Francisco was himself killed, but Retana later found and arrested him.[21]

During that time, following the establishment of the Puerto de Tosanachi, the few Natives there were assigned to the Misión de Cocomorachi. Father Francisco María de Piccolo ministered them. Retana assured the priest that he had instructed the Natives to obey his teachings and attend Holy Mass and prayers.[22]

On January 26, Retana and his men visited Puerto de las Cuebas, where he noted 150 families were living in their homes and tending to their fields. They had constructed a church of the same materials as the pueblo. Near there, at the Pueblo de San Lorenzo, Retana learned that an *hechicero* named Francisco was held prisoner by the pueblo leader, General don Gaspar, because he had killed two Indians and one woman. He killed them by working spells with certain ingredients. At that point, don Gaspar had sent the ingredients to Father Lisarralde so that he could destroy them by burning them. In that way, following the incident, the village was quieted and peaceful.[23]

On January 28, 1692, Retana and his men traveled to Santiago de Babonoiaba. There, they counted 126 peaceful Indians living in the typical thatched-roof houses. As a precaution, the pueblo governor, don Nicolás, keenly aware that some Natives came and went and returned on horseback at night, likely to raid other areas, posted a guard each evening at the entrance to the pueblo as a deterrent to such activity.[24] Retana surmised that anyone leaving the pueblo, even to live in another pueblo or in the sierra, should be punished. Additionally, the soldiers at the nearby posts were watchful of activities at the pueblos of Santa Isabel, San Bernardino, Santa Cruz, San Lorenzo, and Las Cuebas as well as other nearby pueblos such as the Pueblo de San Francisco Xavier de Satebó.[25]

Having reached Satebó, on January 30, 1692, Retana interviewed Governor don Sebastián. He surveyed the pueblo and commented that a guard, similar to that at other pueblos, must be posted at the entrance of the pueblo. Absentee warriors and those given to drunkenness needed to be punished. He urged that Satebó be ready to assist nearby pueblos such as Santiago de Babonoiaba, Joia, and Cuebas. He also demanded that once he was back at his headquarters at Conchos, they communicate any enemy activities to him.[26]

That day, Retana noted that the weather had changed. The harsh winter in that mountainous area had taken much vigor out of his men, not to mention the battered condition of his horses. That day, Retana decided to postpone the rest of his *visitas*. The next day, with a wave of his hand, Retana and his men, knowing that they had accomplished Governor Pardíñas's orders, began to slowly move out to their primary post at the Presidio de San Francisco de Conchos. There, he wrote his report on the successful pacification of the Tarahumara rebellion that had taken place two years earlier.[27]

By February 16, 1692, Governor Pardíñas met with Retana and congratulated him on a job well done. He noted that not only had Retana, as ordered, completed a major part of the reconnaissance of the Provincia de Tarahumares, but he also had reported that all was quiet on that front.[28] Pardíñas furthermore identified certain tribal nations that had rebelled in 1690 but had now sworn obedience to Spain. Among those mentioned were the nations of Tarahumara, Tepehuanes, and Conchos. Retana had also demanded that, if he were still alive, Ignacio Osebac, who they "vulgarly call Ignaciote," and Nicolas del Tuerto be apprehended. The issue was that they had been part of the planning and leadership of the Tarahumara Uprising of 1690–92. Pardíñas needed to be sure of their deaths before he could advise the viceroy of Mexico that the threat was definitely over. If they were dead, then their heads ought to be delivered as proof. Pardíñas then stated that given the testimonies of several witnesses and Retana's reliance on the corresponding letters from Father Joseph Neumann, the Jesuit in the mission district of Sisoguíchi stated that Osebac and Tuerto were indeed dead.[29] Still, an official pronouncement had not been concluded.

Before Pardíñas could make such a conclusion, he needed to review the reports made as early as 1690 from Retana, Father Neumann, and the testimonies of several Tarahumara who had said Osebac was dead and that his and Nicolas de Tuerto's heads had been taken to Parral as proof.

Diligently, Pardíñas reviewed the information given to him by Retana. Rereading Father Neumann's statement, he noted that Osebac was alive at the time and was inciting a new uprising with the people at Tutuaca and Morachi. He noted that Jumari was doing the same with the Tepehuanes. At that time, Pardíñas instructed General don Marcos Fernández de Castañeda, commander at Fronteras de Ostimuri, Thacupeto, and Tepeguanes de la Sierra, to conduct an undercover investigation of don Pablo Jumari by personnel who could observe the actions and movements he was making. They were also to find out whether Osebac was still alive. If the *tlatole* was dead, as testifiers had said, they were to deliver the heads of Osebac and Nicolas el Tuerto. According to Father Neumann, who had received such notice from Father Piccolo, those instructions were met.[30] During that time, Pardíñas was aware of a rumor that Governor don Manuel had said that he thought Osebac could one day be resurrected—a false statement that merely added to the confusion surrounding Osebac's death.[31] Pardíñas, as he had reflected on earlier testimonies, finally concluded that the death of Ignacio Osebac was certain.[32] After one more review, he stated that he no longer doubted that the witnesses had spoken the truth. Pardíñas concluded that the head of Ignaciote Osebac, which was larger than average as he was known to be taller and bigger than most, upon delivery was confirmed to be his.[33]

While the process was slow, given distance and time between gaining knowledge and confirming the death of Osebac and Nicolas el Tuerto, Pardíñas could rest assured that the information gathered in 1690 and confirmed in 1691–92 was accurate: that the leaders of the uprising were dead and that the province could now be secured.

CHAPTER 7

AFTERMATH

In his report of April 20, 1690, Governor Pardíñas explained that the Tarahumara uprising had caused much destruction and damage to structures, including churches, homes, mines, military posts, and farming fields, as well as great suffering to both Spanish settlers and their Indian allies. Beyond the damage to places in Nueva Vizcaya, the Tarahumara and their allies, particularly the Tepehuan and Conchos, had left many dead and had intentionally killed missionary priests throughout the province. Large portions of Nueva Vizcaya lay in ruins.

Given the situation, Pardíñas ordered punitive expeditions throughout the area to punish, subdue, and bring the tribes back into the mission system. Given the large expanse of the province, which included tribes in the difficult terrain of the Sierra Madre Occidental, Pardíñas explained that the initial military response began with the small number of soldiers within the province. Meanwhile, he had requested that the viceroy of Mexico send additional military troops to assist in putting down the rebellion. Initially, the situation throughout Nueva Vizcaya appeared dire. To allay further spread of the rebellion, Governor Pardíñas not only ordered his commanders to perform certain actions; he himself went into the war-torn areas to assess the situation and retake the province from the rebelling nations.

By the early fall of 1690, Governor Pardíñas had also made military *visitas* to a number of Indian villages, such as those named in his reports to Viceroy Conde de Galve in Mexico City.[1] Those villages included Guericarichic, Tomoche, Jesús Carichic, Tairachic, San Joseph de Temaichic, Arisiachi, Pacheras, Papigochi, and Santo Tomás. In that area of the Valle de Papigochi, where he arrived on October 17, he established his camp for the rest of the month. Earlier, in a series of letters to the viceroy written in October 1690, he reported on the state of the pacification process, the specific villages that had been reduced to obedience, as well as the actions his captains had undertaken in order to secure a peaceful province.[2] Putting down the rebellion was one task that he thought had been completed, but the capture of leaders of the rebellion had not been accomplished.[3] That task would be difficult, if not impossible, as many of the leaders and their people had fled to the mountains and deep canyon lands of the Sierra Madre Occidental.

The success that Spanish troops had in putting down the rebellion was owing to the military support by numerous Indian allies (*indios amigos*) who assisted in subduing the Tarahumara warriors and their allies, in particular the Conchos. Even though many of the Tarahumara allies had come from mission sites, *indios amigos* who assisted Spanish soldiers and settlers came from several missions, including Naguerachi, Yepómera, and Papigochi.

A flurry of reports and correspondence was issued by Governor Pardíñas during this time. Following the action in which the rebellion was put down, the governor reported almost daily to the viceroy. In his correspondence, he informed him of military campaigns that he had ordered and noted those that he had personally participated in as he and his men put down the rebellion. At one point, he noted that he had four hundred Indian allies and one hundred Spanish soldiers at his command as well as locations of the military sorties undertaken by him and his officers.

After peace in the region had been achieved, the governor undertook a series of investigations to determine the reasons for the rebellion; the documents include testimonies taken by ladino interpreters from several Indigenous groups who were allies of the Spanish. They also interrogated other warriors who had aligned with the Tarahumara.

In one of his reports, Govern Pardíñas wrote that he had ordered General Retana and General Fernández de la Fuente to make required military *visitas*. Their mission was to assess the pacification of the area as well as to verify that those tribes had remained faithful to the Crown and the Church.

During that time, the Spaniards learned through an informant that the behind-the-scenes leadership of the rebellion came from *tlatlotes*. Andrés Tomás, a ladino, related that at Matachic the *tlatoles* had riled up people to burn the churches and kill the missionaries. While the people at Matachic were quietly leading their lives in late April 1690, a young warrior came into the pueblo and announced that Father Foronda had been killed in Yepómera. Some people fled to the mountains; others were told by a *tlatole* that the time for rebellion was at hand. So well organized were the *tlatoles* that constantly, on a daily basis, they were sending messengers to surrounding tribes encouraging rebellion.[4]

As part of the process of the visits he made at Santo Tomás, where he spent two days, October 17 and 19, Pardíñas interrogated certain Indians regarding rebellion, its leaders, and its causes.[5] At the governor's side were two interpreters, Andrés Tomás and Alonso Muñoz de Sepeda, a criollo who spoke the Tarahumara language. The two interpreters assisted in the cross-examination of Juan Sonora and Domingo, both Spanish-speaking Natives from Matachic; Phelipe Fiscal, also from Matachic; Joseph, the brother of the governor of Yepómera; along with Agustín, Raphael, and Joseph, three men from the village of Naguerachi; Francisco from Matachiqui; and don Juan, the governor of Matachiqui. They all offered valuable information about the causes and early stages of the rebellion that began in November 1689 and was quelled in April 1690. Of particular note to Pardíñas was the information related to the death of Father Diego Ortíz de Foronda, whom they said was killed in Yepómera on March 28 or 29, 1690.

In his investigation of the death of Father Foronda, Pardíñas learned that rebellious Indians had also destroyed the milpas (cornfields) near the missions. Information learned by "ladinos," that is, acculturated Indians fluent in Spanish, assisted the interrogation efforts. The use of ladino interpreters proved invaluable in interrogating various informants. They noted that the Spanish justified harsh treatment in assaulting the rebel Indians because they believed that the Tarahumara and Concho warriors were barbaric.[6] They assisted in the interviews of certain Indian governors who detailed the death of Father Foronda. They said that there was great resentment toward the priest because of the hard work, by force, he imposed on them to make adobe blocks for the construction of the mission church at Yepómera.

On this particular inspection of Nueva Vizcaya, which had been hit hard in the rebellion, Governor Pardíñas continued his investigation into the immediate causes of the rebellion that had caused much destruction and death. During his investigation, he had several people interrogated. One of them was Governor Antonio of Yepómera. In relating his account as to what caused the rebellion, he recalled that in tears, he had warned Father Foronda that certain warriors, in great numbers, were coming to kill him in his home that very night. Father Foronda refused to believe him. Governor Antonio urged him to leave with the two Spanish escorts, Teniente Juan de Urias and a settler, Francisco Fondes, who would also be killed. The warriors were Tarahumara from Naguerachi. Governor Antonio said that those Indians had refused to be missionized. One of their leaders, known as "Joseph," refused to be dissuaded and threatened to kill Governor Antonio and his comrade, but they fled. The rebels set fire to the rooftops of the houses, including that of Father Foronda, as the two escorts fired four shots from their arquebuses, killing one of the rebel leaders. Swinging their swords, they were killed by the many arrows fired at them by the bowmen. Meanwhile, Father Foronda tried to leave his burning building. As he ran out the doorway, he was hit by many arrows. While on the ground, he was hit many times by the warriors and finally he was clubbed to death.[7] Having witnessed the violence, Governor Antonio fled to Matachic and warned his people to flee to the mountains. He did not go with them but later learned that most had fled. Governor Antonio encountered some soldiers and warned them of the rebellion. He soon returned to the land of war with them.

Governor Antonio testified that the rebellion was captained by a one-eyed Indian from Naguerachi called Nicolás. At the start of the rebellion, Nicolás and his son attacked some homes and killed an old man named Coarachi. Nicolás commanded the rebellion as it spread to Naguerachi, Sirupa, Aboreachic, Pasacheachic, and Garaguasachic. In all those places, the churches were pillaged and burned.[8]

Governor Pardíñas had wanted to know the immediate cause that had precipitated the rebellion. In so doing, he at last learned of the final moments of Father Foronda and his death's possible role in causing the rebellion. Reviewing his information, Pardíñas noted that one informant, Ignacio Osebac, whose Native name was Ygnasiote, had said that when the old man, Coarachi, and his son, among others, were killed, he and others were hiding. He testified that he knew the causes of the attack. He said that he had heard of the discontent with Father Foronda, particularly among the Conchos, who were living at Chiguichupa. They were taken to the mission at Yepómera. There, Father Foronda made them make adobe blocks, and even though he promised to pay them by giving them one or two cows, they were never paid. So they returned and took cattle to Queparipa. They also took some mission Indians from Yepómera. Father Foronda dispatched some loyal Indians from Yepómera to get them back. He did this because the governor was not there to do so at the spur of the moment. One of the loyal Indians, Juan Caporal, with fourteen others, surprised a group of Conchos and captured four Conchos men; one young boy; five women, one of them elderly; and a six- or eight-year-old boy. The captives were taken to Father Foronda, who dispatched four of the men and the elderly woman to the mission at Cosiguriachi. The woman escaped en route. It was thought that she had hastened to warn that the *tlatoles* had planned against Father Foronda and the loyal Indians at Yepómera. Father Foronda, throughout that time, had remained with the three captive women and the little boy. The women fled, leaving the boy behind. The night Father Foronda was killed, the boy was with him. The Conchos took the boy with them.[9] Ignacio left his interrogators with a chilling observation.

The informant, however, focused on another cause for the rebellion. It seemed that the Conchos knew that Father Foronda "abhorred" them. They said that he often had soldiers punish Natives from Naguerachi by hustling them off to Yepómera. They said the soldiers even had a document that would allow them to behead them or hang them. Knowing that Father Foronda was behind the soldiers being sent to their village, they openly declared that they would kill the priest. "Let the soldiers come to behead us" was one of their cries. They decried that Father Foronda saw them as evil people and enemies who refused to hear the Holy Mass or accept the teachings of the Church.[10]

The informant was asked if the Indians at Yepómera and Naguerachi had issues with the Spanish settlers or if they had taken herds, corn, horses, chickens, or other things, or if the *alcalde mayor* of Cosiguriachi had caused them anger or had taken, by force, or burned their *jacales*, cornfields, or other things. He responded that the settlers had never come to trade or purchase anything as it was too far for them to travel. Neither had the *alcalde mayor* of Cosiguriachi ever gone to Yepómera or Naguerachi. They had no complaints against the settlers because they do not go there.[11] Still, the situation regarding how the tribes felt about the Spanish intrusion had not and would not change for the rest of the seventeenth century.

While the rebellions of the past decades appeared to have been a part of the past, the situation had not actually cooled. There were many incidents throughout the missions, settlements, mines, and trade routes that proved troublesome to Spanish officials. Both settlers and missionaries asked for more military presence in their areas. Spanish officials felt that such presence merely inspired more resentment among the tribes. The missions appeared to be a hot spot to the new threats that were beginning to mount. There were many anti-mission incidents throughout Nueva Vizcaya. For example, just as the situation with the Tarahumara was appearing peaceful, a new disturbance arose. It appears that Father Gaspare Sanna at the mission at Teméychi preached a message about a false god that riled up the *hechiceros* there and at the adjoining mission sites. Teméychi comprised four pueblos and a *visita* at Nuestra Señora del Pópulo los Álamos.[12]

Several times, the Tarahumara fearing reprisals picked up and left for a mountain refuge. The Jesuits in several missions, hoping to bring the tribes to accept Christianity, argued that the Indians had abandoned the one true God. When Father Sanna had to go to Cusihuiríachi to deal with issues raised by Spanish settlers, the Indians at a nearby village called Poacher rushed in fury against Teméychi, protesting the preachings of the priest, and attempted to burn down the church and the priest's residence. The mission Indians at Teméychi repelled them and put out the fire but a woman witness said that at a distance she could see the fire at Teméychi and believed that the church was still ablaze. The priest at a nearby mission at Carichí sent out two people to see what was going on. They returned and said that the rebels had attempted to burn down the church and Father Sanna's home.[13]

But the issue was still troublesome. From a distant mission site, for example, villagers could see the bright firelight from a large kiln to heat and dry the adobe block located at the mission at Tajfrachi. Surrounding villages, almost in panic, thought that the church at Teméychi was burning.[14] Fearing reprisal from the rebels or the Spanish military, some fled their villages.

Still, most believed that the attack was largely provoked by Father Sanna's preaching. It was obvious, wrote Father Neumann, that the people at Teméychi could no longer support the priest. They warned that if the Father Superior did not relieve Father Sanna, rebellion was the solution. Meanwhile, Church officials told Father Sanna, still at Cusihuiríachi, not to return to Teméychi.[15]

Having learned about the attacks, the missionary priest at Carichí sent two people out to see what had actually happened at Teméychi. He learned that the people were upset with Father Sanna's messages that attacked their Native beliefs. During that time, 1697 to 1698, violence was pervasive as several missions suffered similar rebellions. For example, the mission churches at Tomochi and Arisćachi were set on fire by the rebels.[16]

Spanish settlers spread the alarm to Spanish officials. Given the threat of a rebellion, General Retana was sent to Papigochi to suppress the leaders of a possible planned rebellion. As word of Retana's presence in the area spread to other places, panic of suppression flashed among the tribes, especially among many of the villagers at Pachera, who had been involved in a similar conspiracy. They fled the missions to their mountain sanctuaries, free from the influence of the missionaries. Retana debated whether to pursue the fugitive rebels and attack them or try to persuade them to agree to a peace between them. Governor Pardíñas told him to remain in Papigochi and send out scouts to determine what the fugitive rebels planned. But the rebels stayed put in their mountain sanctuaries. They had plenty of food, water, and arrows in case they would be attacked by Retana.[17] Upon receiving the new intelligence, Pardíñas next ordered Retana to take his Indian allies and one hundred soldiers to engage the rebels wherever found. Retana wasted no time and soon entered the Sierra de Guébachi and surrounding deep canyon areas in pursuit of the rebels.[18]

The terrain was unforgiving. There, at a high escarpment with large boulders, Retana met the rebel warriors.[19] Given the high walls of the rock escarpment, Retana's men could not scale the escarpment; the only way was to go around through a very narrow passageway, which was obstructed by large boulders. At that point, the rebels were too far away even for musket balls from Spanish weapons to reach them.[20]

Given the danger in which it would put his men, Retana retreated to a lower place near a small river, where he laid siege to the escarpment and waited for the rebels, who would run out of food and water, to surrender. Meanwhile, his soldiers were stationed in small guard units all around the escarpment, blocking any exit the rebels could take without an open battle. Seeing the split command, the rebels, with a great shout that could be heard from a distance, attacked one of the units, killing the soldiers. At that very moment, Retana and his officers were having lunch and, hearing the shouts, scrambled for their weapons and horses. They attacked the rebels, putting them in flight back to their boulder sanctuary. Retana could not attack the position of the rebel sanctuary so he ordered his troops to retreat to their former camps.[21] At that point, Retana, considering that the rebels were entrenched in a difficult place for him to attack, saw no value in remaining stationary as heavy rains drenched the area and forced him to return to Papigochi.[22]

As the campaign at Papigochi faded away, the Tobosos raided trade caravans, settlements, ranches, and farms. The missionaries complained to the viceroy about the lack of military security in Nueva Vizcaya.[23] Still, the Spanish military continued to press the rebels wherever possible.

There were other instances where *hechiceros* were captured and sentenced to be executed by Retana. In one case, at a mission called Sohuíarachi, which was a *visita* of the main mission at San Francisco de Borja at Taguéachi, lived a "diabolic" *hechicero,* a practitioner of black magic. He was accused of crimes and bad deeds done by others. Retana captured him and ordered his execution. But the missionary Jesuit Francisco de Celada pleaded that he not be executed but sentenced to a life of labor at the *moline de metales,* the iron mill, near the main mission.[24]

As it turned out, Father Celada's sentiment for the "diabolic" *hechicero* changed when it was discovered that his black magic had resulted in the death of a young girl. Her mother told Father Celada about the evil done to her daughter.[25] In the end, the *hechicero* was executed. There were other instances where Jesuit missionaries accused *hechiceros* of similar crimes.[26]

The situation appeared to be out of control when the Indians tried to use Retana, still at Papigochi, to execute certain *hechiceros,* who they blamed for the deaths of certain pueblo villagers. On June 28, 1697, for example, certain Indian villagers demanded that Retana arrest and punish a woman *hechicera,* whom they accused of killing certain captured Indians that she had executed and decapitated. Her father, an *hechicero,* had, according to Father Neumann, taught her the art of black magic. Her own people accused her of murdering many people in their villages. Retana refused to be drawn into a private and local situation by arresting and executing her. He told them that she was their problem. That rebuff angered the villagers. In another incident, the Indians sentenced a different woman to undergo an "ordeal by fire" for her crimes. They became even more enraged when the priests refused to condemn the accused wrongdoers and instead offered to comfort them.[27] It appeared to them that Retana's and the priests' attitudes were contradictory to their duties to protect all of them against wrongdoers. Those and other incidents apparently triggered a series of revengeful attacks on Spanish settlements.[28] Such incidents had become commonplace as unrest continued to build up again in Nueva Vizcaya.

In the end, the immediate causes of the uprising, in Pardíñas's mind, bore repetition. In his correspondence to the viceroy, he described the events that had resulted in the death of Father Foronda. Basically, the immediate cause revolved around the resentment against the priest and his actions. Pardíñas's conclusions were not baseless. Accordingly, many witnesses described the Jesuit's death; a number of their testimonies were presented in his presence, which led him to conclude that Father Foronda's murder was the spark that fueled the rebellion. Another Jesuit killed during the initial stages of the rebellion was identified as Padre Manuel Sanches. Nicolás el Tuerto was identified as one of his murderers. These facts would be repeated in much of the documentation following the final rebellion of the seventeenth century, the Tarahumara rebellion of 1690.

New issues cropped up. Just at the end of the seventeenth century, silver was discovered in Chihuahua, not far to the east from Cusihuiríachi, which was considered to be one of the richest mining areas. New settlers poured into the area. Miners from other poorer areas abandoned their mines and went to Chihuahua, a growing town that, later, was officially founded in 1709. Soon, missionaries followed.[29]

By the start of the eighteenth century, new uprisings were again in flux as the focus shifted largely to the general area of Chihuahua and the rest of Nueva Vizcaya was again beset with rebellions.[30] As the seventeenth century gave way to the eighteenth century, the situation had not changed. By the early 1720s, Nueva Vizcaya and other nearby provinces faced a new cycle of rebellions.[31]

Indeed, Spanish officials concluded that the rebellions were not isolated cases. Following each rebellion, Spanish investigators realized that such rebellions were part of a larger picture. The historical examination of the Tepehuan Revolt of 1616, for example, hinted that some Native rebellions were linked to events elsewhere in northern New Spain. Sixty-four years before the Pueblo Revolt of 1680, the Tepehuan Revolt of 1616 began in November in Sinaloa south of Tarahumara country. While the Tepehuan warriors' well-planned assault sent settlers, miners, and missionaries scurrying for safety, all but destroying the Jesuit mission system in their homeland for several years, Spanish officials found that there were outside influences for the rebellion, including that of an Indian from New Mexico who had urged the rebellion. During six decades of warfare, many men, women, and children died on both sides, as large-scale destruction took place. The Tarahumara, the Tepehuan, and other tribes in northern New Spain held tight to their convictions regarding intrusions onto their lands. They had also strived to drive out intruders from their homelands.

Throughout the Spanish colonial period, varied opinions persisted among settlers and officials about the causes of widespread warfare throughout the area. In New Mexico, for example, some Spanish militarists expressed sympathetic views, which reasonably applied to other provinces such as Chihuahua, Sonora, and Coahuila, about attacks made by local tribes on Spanish and Pueblo settlements and speculated on the reasons for their raids. Of the more enlightened attitudes, for example, some Spanish officials explained that the Apache's aggressive behavior was a response to intruders on their lands rather than an expression of innate violent character in Apache people. They agreed that the Apache waged war against settlers and miners because they trespassed on their tribal lands and exploited the people and the resources of the land. Some explained that the Apache robbed settlers because hunting alone did not support their needs. In the eighteenth century, Bernardo de Galvéz, a military commander, wrote, "If the Indian is no friend, it is because he owes us no kindness, and . . . if he avenges himself it is for just satisfaction of his grievances." In 1799, Viceroy Antonio de Bucareli confided to José de Galvéz, the intendant general of New Spain, "An impartial judge could . . . see [that] every charge we might make against them would be offset by as many crimes committed by our side."[32]

On the other hand, Spanish officials and settlers did not fail to understand their own role in provoking war with the tribes, but in the wake of a devastating raid, the reasons for the provocations did not matter. Still, each side justified its reasons for war against the other. Such reactions were not exclusive to Spanish settlers but were also found among other European settlers and miners throughout North America and the Caribbean who came to the area as late as the mid-nineteenth century.

APPENDIX

Seventeenth-Century Nueva Vizcaya Place-Names

A: Atotonilco*, Aguascalientes, Avino, (Villa de) Aguilar, Ariséachi

B: Batopilas, Bolsón de Mapimí, Bocas*, (Los) Berrios, Balleza, (San Francisco de) Borja, Bachimba

C: Chihuahua, Camino Real de Tierra Adentro, Coahuila, Cuencamé, Cusihuiríachi (Cosiguriachi), Cuautitlán, Ciénega*, Cuicillo* (9 leagues from Zacatecas), Cerro Gordo, Chalchihuites, Chínipas, Caricha (Jesús Carichic), Carichí, Cajurichi, Cocomóraci, Chiguichupa

D: Durango

E: Encinillas, El Paso del Norte

F: Fresnillo

G: Guanajuato, Guarisamey, Gavilanes, Gran Chichimeca, Gracián, Guazapares (Montañas de), Guericarichic, (Sierra de) Guébachi

H: Huejotitlan

I: Indé

J: Jilotepec, Jofre*, Jasó*

L: La Sauceda, Las Bocas, La Mohina, Llerena, Lagos, La Punta

M: Mexico City, Michoacán, Maxcala*, (San Juan de) Meziquital, Matachi, Matachic, Matachiqui

N: New Mexico (Santa Fe, San Juan de los Caballeros, San Gabriel), Nueva Vizcaya (Nieto Pass, Nombre de Díos, Nieves: Real de Minas de Nieves), Naguerachi

O: Ojuelos*
P: Parral (San José de Parral), Papigochi, Pichacho, Portezuelo*, Palmillas*, Portezuelo
Q: Querétaro
R: Río de los Sauces, Río Florido, Río Conchos
S: San Luis Potosí, Sinaloa, Santiago, Sierra Madre Occidental, Sierra Madre Oriental, Sonora, Saltillo, San Dimas, San Diego, Santa Bárbara, San Juan del Río, San Luis de la Paz, San Felipe, San Miguel, San Martín, San Bartolomé, Sombrerete, San Joaquín (Real de), San Juan de Mezquital, San Pablo de Tepehuanes, San Javier de Satebó, San Jerónimo Huejotitlan, San Bernabé, Sisoguíchi
T: Texas, Torreón, Tenerapa, Tunal, Tenerapa, Tayolita, Tepejí, Teméichi (Teméychi), Tomochi, Tomache, Titiana, Tajfrachi
V: Valle de Guadiana (Durango), Valle de Papigochi, Ventanas, Villa Escobedo, Villa de Aguascalientes, Valle de Sushi, Valle de Poanas
Y: Yepómera
Z: Zacatecas

* Presidios at Maxcala, Jofre, Atotonilco, Jasó, Portezuelo, Ciénega Grande, Cuicillo, Palmillas, Ojuelos, and Bocas
Source: Spanish Colonial Research Center (SCRC) file folder.

NOTES

Introduction

1. Angie Debo, *Geronimo: The Man, His Time, His Place* (University of Oklahoma Press, 1976), 420.
2. Joseph P. Sánchez, "Indigenous Territoriality and European Sovereignty in the Early Centuries of European Discovery of and Claim to North America," *New Mexico Historical Review* 95, no. 2 (Spring 2020): 213–27.
3. See Joseph P. Sánchez, "Old Heat and New Light on Spanish Diplomacy Regarding the Louisiana Purchase and the Defense of New Mexico, 1762–1819," *Louisiana History* 64, no. 1 (Winter 2023): 5–43. It should also be noted that treaties between France, Spain, and England in the early 1760s stated that Indian boundaries marked by rivers would be respected. Still, while those attitudes prevailed, Spain, England, and France, during the travails of the Seven Years' War and the treaties that followed, inclusive of the Treaty of Paris of 1763, openly acknowledged the territorial rights of tribes within the area that would be known as the Louisiana Purchase. Within the next phase of the history of the Louisiana Purchase, Spain proposed a Treaty of Friendship (Tratado de Amistad), which later became the basis of the Adams-Onis Treaty of 1819. Also, Pinckney's Treaty of 1795 had dealt with the treatment of Native tribes whose territories were marked by rivers that had formed the Spanish–English boundary and the way in which the boundary line would be set. Both Spain and England, as in previous treaties, had maintained that Indian territoriality based on river roundaries should be respected. As referenced in the draft of the Tratado de Amistad, José Pizzaro and other Spanish diplomats stated that "peace and good harmony between the diverse nations of Indians, who live

along the torrents adjacent to boundaries drawn by rivers as mentioned in previous articles," should be observed and respected. See Official Spanish Draft of the Tratado de Amistad issued for review to the king of Spain by Ministro Plenipotenciario to the U.S., don José Pizzaro, Washington, D.C., April 8, 1817, Archivo Histórico Nacional, Madrid, Spain, Estado 5641, fols. 70–71.

4. See Kent McNeil, "The Louisiana Purchase: Indian and American Sovereignty in the Missouri Watershed," *Western Historical Quarterly* 50, no. 1 (2019): 17–42.
5. Andrés Pérez de Ribas, *History of the Triumphs of Our Holy Faith Among the Most Barbarous and Fierce Peoples of the New World,* trans. Daniel T. Reff, Maureen Ahern, and Richard Danford (University of Arizona Press, 1999), 589.
6. Pérez de Ribas, *History of the Triumphs,* 592.
7. Pérez de Ribas, *History of the Triumphs,* 589.
8. Pérez de Ribas, *History of the Triumphs,* 591–92.
9. Pérez de Ribas, *History of the Triumphs,* 637.
10. Florence C. Lister and Robert H. Lister, *Chihuahua: Storehouse of Storms* (University of New Mexico Press, 1966), 30.
11. José de la Cruz Pacheco Rojas, *Milenarismo tepehuán: Mesianismo y resistencia indígena en el norte novohispano* (Siglo XXI Editores, 2008), 110. See also Pérez de Ribas, *History of the Triumphs,* 595.
12. Pacheco Rojas, *Milenarismo tepehuán,* 109–10. Pacheco writes, "Es conveniente señalar que el fraile Andrés de Heredia había tenido conocimiento de que los indios de las misiones jesuitas vecinas a Topia estaban preparanto la guerra contra los españoles poco antes del gran levantamiento de 1616. Él mismo había hecho del conocimiento del gobernador Gaspar de Alvea sobre los *tlatoles* que circulaban en torno del convento, por lo cual contribuyó con poco más de cien guerreros acaxees en apoyo de las fuerzas españolas" (109n38).
13. Pacheco Rojas, *Milenarismo tepehuán,* 110–11.
14. Pacheco Rojas, *Milenarismo tepehuán,* 111.
15. Pacheco Rojas, *Milenarismo tepehuán,* 111.
16. Pérez de Ribas, *History of the Triumphs,* 595.
17. Pérez de Ribas, *History of the Triumphs,* 594–95.
18. Pacheco Rojas, *Milenarismo tepehuán,* 114.
19. Sánchez, "Indigenous Territoriality," 8.
20. Joseph Neumann, *Historia de las rebeliones en la sierra tarahumara (1626–1724),* ed. Luis González Rodríguez, trans. Joaquín Díaz Anchondo and Luis González Rodríguez, Colección Centenario 8 (Editorial Camino, 1991), 145.
21. See "Chihuahuan Desert," Wikipedia, accessed June 20, 2023, https://en.wikipedia.org/wiki/Chihuahuan_Desert.
22. Highest Mountain Peaks in Chihuahua: 1. Cerro Mohinora, 3,300 m (prom: 811 m); 2. Cerro Las Iglesias, 3,101 m (prom: 406 m); 3. La Jara, 3,062 m (prom: 802 m); 4. Ojo la Yegua, 3,026 m (prom: 100 m); 5. Cerro El Alto de San Jose, 2,981 m (prom: 166 m); 6. Rumurachi, 2,980 m (prom: 541 m); 7. Cerro El Alto de Las Garrochas, 2,969 m (prom: 246 m); 8. Cerro La Culebra, 2,960 m (prom:

823 m); 9. La Bandera, 2,959 m (prom: 316 m). Other Prominent Mountains: 10. Cerro Cumbre de Los Metates, 2,475 m (prom: 1,078 m); 11. Cerro Grande, 2,295 m (prom: 936 m); 12. Cerro Las Higueras Sierra las Candelarias, 2,141 m (prom: 843 m); 13. Cerro El Pinole, 2,898 m (prom: 841 m); 14. Cerro La Culebra, 2,960 m (prom: 823 m); 15. Cerro Mohinora, 3,300 m (prom: 811 m); 16. La Jara, 3,062 m (prom: 802 m); 17. Cerro Grande, 2,539 m (prom: 802 m); 18. Cerro El Molino, 1,940 m (prom: 800 m); 19. "Mountains of Chihuahua," PeakVisor, accessed June 20, 2023, https://peakvisor.com/adm/chihuahua.html.

23. See Roland H. Wauer and David H. Riskind, eds., *Transactions of the Symposium on the Biological Resources of the Chihuahuan Desert Region: United States and Mexico*, Transactions and Precedence's Series 3 (U.S. Department of the Interior, National Park Service), 1977.
24. "The Mammogy," Session II; "Botany," Session III; "Ichthyofauna," Session IV; "Herpetogauna," Session V; and "Avefauna," Session VI, in Wauer and Riskind, *Transactions of the Symposium*, 127–616.

Chapter 1

1. Historiography is the study of how history is written, by whom, and the factors that influence the purpose of its rendition. Often, themes on particular histories are frequently repeated by other authors and influence succeeding publications until new approaches to the same theme are reconsidered in future publications. The writing of history is based on critical assessments, such as a multifactor analysis approach, as well as the selection of particular details based on documentary sources that apply to an evolving theme within the framework of the historical process. The writing of history may also include quoting the works of other historians or repeating their thesis statements, which often occurs many times over by other historians repeating the same information without further analytical efforts. That is, often, an idea is accepted and repeated until someone comes up with documentation that changes or refutes a particular theme, notion, or thesis. Historical writing is based on assessing events that evolve from a historical process. I define the historical process as an occurrence, a state or phenomenon that has to do with the evolution of an idea or concept that ties to an event or a series of events. The historical process is a function of the relationships within and interactions of the affairs of humankind with time, events, the sequence and continuities of events, causes, effects, and the change or changes that develop as a consequence. The historical process may provide directionality. In summary, the historical process is evident in the questions who are we, where do we come from, and where are we going? In the historical dialectic, the historical process is best defined as an unanswerable paradox that can never be completed because it is something that is in a perpetual state of becoming.
2. Neumann, *Historia de las rebeliones*, 39.
3. Andrés Cavo, *Historia de México* (1836; repr., Editorial Patria, 1949). Originally written in the eighteenth century, it was first published in 1836. Libro Noveno

includes a section on the Tarahumara rebellion of 1689–90. For a biography of Father Cavo, see "Andrés Cavo," Wikipedia, accessed June 27, 2023, https://www.wikiwand.com/en/Andr%C3%A9s_Cavo. See also Andrés Cavo, *Historia de México* (Universidad Autónoma de México, 2013).

4. Hubert Howe Bancroft, *History of the North Mexican States and Texas*, 2 vols., vols. 15 and 16 of *The Works of Hubert Howe Bancroft* (A. L. Bancroft, 1884); see chapter 5 in vol. 2 regarding the history of Nueva Vizcaya.
5. Bancroft, *History of the North Mexican States and Texas*, 321.
6. Pérez de Ribas, *History of the Triumphs*, 595.
7. Alonso de la Mota y Escobar, *Descripción geográfica de los reinos de Nueva Galicia, Nueva Vizcaya y Nueva León*, ed. Joaquín Ramírez Cabañas (Editorial Pedro Robredo, 1940).
8. Roberto Mario Salmón, *Indian Revolts in Northern New Spain: A Synthesis of Resistance, 1680–1786* (University Press of America, 1991).
9. Ysla Campbell, ed., *El Contacto entre los españoles e indígenas en el norte de Nueva España* (Universidad Autónoma de Ciudad Juárez, 1992).
10. Ernest J. Burrus and Félix Zubillaga, trans. and eds., *El noroeste de México: Documentos sobre las misiones jesuitas, 1600–1769* (Universidal Nacional Autónoma de Mexico, 1986).
11. Peter Masten Dunne, S.J., *Early Jesuit Missions in Tarahumara* (University of California Press, 1948).
12. See, for example, Francisco Javier Alegre, *Historia de la provincia de la Compañía de Jesús de Nueva España*, ed. Ernest J. Burrus and Félix Zubillaga, new ed., 4 vols. (Institutum Historicum, 1956–1960). See also Adolph Francis Alphonse Bandelier, *A History of the Southwest: A Study of the Civilization and Conversion of the Indians in Southwestern United States and Northwestern Mexico from the Earliest Times to 1700*, ed. Ernest J. Burrus (Biblioteca Apostolica Vaticana, 1969). These two volumes relate a broader history of the Jesuit missionary efforts, inclusive of those in the Tarahumara missionary field, which ended with their expulsion from the Spanish Empire in 1767.
13. Luis González Rodríguez, *El noroeste novohispano en la época colonial* (Universidad Nacional Autónoma de México, 1993).
14. Thomas E. Sheridan and Thomas H. Naylor, *Rarámuri: A Tarahumara Colonial Chronicle, 1607–1791* (Northland Press, 1979).
15. Thomas H. Naylor and Charles W. Polzer, S.J., eds., *The Presidio and Militia on the Northern Frontier of New Spain: A Documentary History*, 2 vols. (University of Arizona Press, 1986).
16. Susan M. Deeds, *Defiance and Deference in Mexico's Colonial North: Indians Under Spanish Rule in Nueva Vizcaya* (University of Texas Press, 2003).
17. Hubert Howe Bancroft, *History of the North Mexican States*, vol. 1, 334–35.
18. Charles W. Polzer, S.J., *Rules and Precepts of the Jesuit Missions of Northwestern New Spain* (University of Arizona Press, 1979), 9.

19. Susan Deeds, *Defiance and Deference in Mexico's Colonial North*; Bancroft, *History of the North Mexican States*, 1:313. Bancroft mentions the smallpox epidemic of 1608. Another issue mentioned by Bancroft was the drought and famine resulting in food shortages that hit the area in 1813. Bancroft writes, "In former times drought had ever been productive of war for the possession of the deepest holes with their fish supply, but Christianity had changed all that" (314).
20. Susan M. Deeds, "Indigenous Responses to Mission Settlement in Nueva Vizcaya," in *The New Latin American Mission History*, ed. Erick Langer and Robert H. Jackson (University of Nebraska Press, 1995).
21. Allan Christelow, "Father Joseph Neumann, Jesuit Missionary to the Tarahumares," *Hispanic American Historical Review* 19, no. 4 (1939): 423–42.
22. Roberto Mario Salmón, "Tarahumara Resistance to Mission Congregation in Northern New Spain, 1580–1710," *Ethnohistory* 24, no. 4 (1977): 379–93.

Chapter 2

1. Lister and Lister, *Chihuahua*, 10–11.
2. See Joseph P. Sánchez, María Luisa Pérez González, and Bruce A. Erickson, "Toward a Definition of the Spanish Camino Real: Cabañas, Villas, Armies and the Spanish Crown," in *From Mexico City to Santa Fe: A Historical Guide to El Camino Real de Tierra Adentro*, comp. Joseph P. Sánchez and Bruce A. Erickson (Río Grande Books, 2011), 262–68.
3. *Recopilación de las Leyes de los Reinos de las Indias* (Ediciones Cultura Hispánica, 1973), Tomo Segundo, Ley II, Libro IV, Título VI.
4. See *Recopilación de las Leyes de los Reinos de las Indias*, Tomo Segundo. For examples, see *Que cerca de las Reducciones no haya estancias de Ganado*, Ley XX, Libro VI, Título III; *Que entre los Indios no vivan Españoles, Mestizos, ni Mulatos*, Ley XXI, Libro VI, Título III; *Que entre los Indios no vivan Españoles, Mestizos, ni Mulatos aunque hayan comprador tierras den los Pueblos* (living in pueblos was prohibited), Ley XXII, Libro VI, Título III; *Que no se den tierras en perjuicio de los Indios, y las dadas se vuelvan a sus dueños*, Ley IX, Libro IV, Título XII; *Que las estancias para ganados se den apartados de Pueblos y Sementaras de Indios*, Lay XII, Libro IV, Título XII.
5. *Recopilación de las Leyes de los Reinos de las Indias*, Tomo Segundo, Libro IV, Título VII, Ley IX, fol. 91. Spanish town councils or town halls predated those of the English such as the New England Town Meeting (1620) by more than a century.
6. *Recopilación de las Leyes de los Reinos de las Indias*, Tomo Segundo, Libro IV, Título IX, Ley XIII (published in 1680), fols. 97–98.
7. Cabildo de San Gabriel, 1603, Biblioteca Nacional de Antropología e Historia, Mexico City, Mexico, Serie Documentos, CA 199.
8. Spanish cabildos (town councils) in the Spanish Empire preceded, by more than a century, those in the English Thirteen Colonies, where the first town councils

were established in Virginia's House of Burgesses in 1619 and the New England Town Meeting in 1620.

9. Joseph P. Sánchez, *Pueblos, Plains, and Province: New Mexico in the Seventeenth Century* (University Press of Colorado, 2021), 13.
10. Sánchez, *Pueblos, Plains, and Province*, 13.
11. Sánchez, *Pueblos, Plains, and Province*, 13.
12. Sánchez, *Pueblos, Plains, and Province*, 13.
13. Philip Wayne Powell, *Soldiers, Indians and Silver: The Northward Advance of New Spain, 1550–1600* (University of California Press, 1969), 17–18. Also note that the Spanish league, particularly in the eighteenth century, is generally reckoned to be 2.6 miles. Travelers were often surprisingly accurate in their measurement of distance traveled in a day.
14. Sánchez and Erickson, *From Mexico City to Santa Fe*, 74.
15. Joseph P. Sánchez and Bruce A. Erickson, comps., *From Saltillo, Mexico, to San Antonio and East Texas: An Historical Guide to El Camino Real de Tierra Afuera and El Camino Real de lo Jujus During the Spanish Colonial Period* (Rio Grande Press, 2016), 293–300. The antiquity and dynamics of Spanish legal tradition and practices were based on Greco-Roman traditions. See also Joseph P. Sánchez, *El Camino Real de California: From Ancient Pathways to Modern Byways* (University of New Mexico Press, 2019), 3.
16. Modesto Bargalló, *La minería y metalurgía en la América española durante la época colonial* (Fondo de Cultura Económica, 1955), 294.
17. Bargalló, *La minería y metalurgía en la América española*, 56.
18. *Recopilación de las Leyes de los Reinos de las Indias*, Tomo Segundo, Libro IV, Título XIX, Ley II, fol. 118. The precedents for the law had been established earlier and recent citations include the date November 14, 1515.
19. *Recopilación de las Leyes de los Reinos de las Indias*, Tomo Segundo, Libro IV, Título XIX, Ley III, fol. 118.
20. *Recopilación de las Leyes de los Reinos de las Indias*, Tomo Segundo, Libro IV, Título XIX, Ley XIII, fol. 120.
21. *Recopilación de las Leyes de los Reinos de las Indias*, Tomo Segundo, Libro IV, Título XIX, Ley XII, fol. 120.
22. *Recopilación de las Leyes de los Reinos de las Indias*, Tomo Segundo, Libro IV, Título XX, Ley Primera, fol. 120.
23. Bargalló, *La minería y metalurgía en la América española*, 65. See also Francisco R. Almada, *Diccionario de historia, geografía y Biografía chihuahuenses* (Ediciones del Azar, 1928), 2:285. However, Almada wrote that silver had been discovered in Santa Bárbara in 1564.
24. J. Lloyd Mecham, *Francisco de Ibarra y la Nueva Vizcaya*, trans. Víctor Meneguzzo Peruzzo (Universidad Juárez de Estado de Durango, 2005), 138.
25. Herbert E. Bolton, ed., *Spanish Exploration in the Southwest, 1542–1706* (Charles Scribner's Sons, 1916), 201.
26. Bolton, *Spanish Exploration*, 201.

27. Sánchez, *Pueblos, Plains, and Province*, 53.
28. Sánchez, *Pueblos, Plains, and Province*, 59.
29. François Chevalier, *Land and Society in Colonial Mexico: The Great Hacienda* (University of California Press, 1963), 266.

Chapter 3

1. Lister and Lister, *Chihuahua*, 35.
2. Genealogia de Nicolás de Aguilar, May 8, 1663, Proceso contra Aguilar, 1661–1665, Archivo General de la Nación, Mexico City, Mexico, Sección Inquisición 512.
3. Causa de denunciación por querella que dió Nicolas de Aguilar contra Sebastian de la Canal y otras personas sobre averlo derrumbado un pilar de su mina, March 11, 1641, Archivo Histórico de Parral, Parral, Mexico, Sección Causas Criminales, año 1641.
4. Causa criminal contra Nicolás de Aguilar por homicidio cometido en la persona de Germando de Villagomez en San Diego de Minas Nuevas, Archivo Histórico de Parral, Sección Causas Criminales, año 1654.
5. Causa criminal contra Nicolás de Aguilar.
6. Causa criminal contra Nicolás de Aguilar.
7. Causa criminal contra Nicolás de Aguilar.
8. Descargo de Acusaciones hecho por Nicolás de Aguilar, Capítulos 42 and 44, Proceso contra Aguilar, 1661–1665, Archivo General de la Nación, Sección Inquisición 512.
9. Descargo de Acusaciones hecho por Nicolás de Aguilar, Capítulos 42 and 44.
10. Capitulaciones, Capítulo 75, Proceso contra Mendizabal, 1663, Archivo General de la Nación, Sección Inquisición 594.
11. The entire Inquisition case against Nicolás de Aguilar is found in Proceso contra Aguilar, 1661–1665, Archivo General de la Nación, Sección Inquisición 512. See also Declaración del Capitán Miguel de Noriega, Mexico, October 3, 1661; and Descargo de Acusaciones hecho por Nicolás de Aguilar, Capítulo 42, Proceso contra Aguilar, Archivo General de la Nación, Sección Inquisitión 512, fol. 118.
12. Neumann, *Historia de las rebeliones*, 18.
13. Neumann, *Historia de las rebeliones*, 18–19.
14. Neumann, *Historia de las rebeliones*, 19–20.
15. Neumann, *Historia de las rebeliones*, 21.
16. Neumann, *Historia de las rebeliones*, 24.
17. Neumann, *Historia de las rebeliones*, 29n 1.
18. Lister and Lister, *Chihuahua*, 32–33.
19. Lister and Lister, *Chihuahua*, 39.
20. Bishop de la Mota y Escobar was born in Mexico City on May 18, 1546, of Captain Gerónimo Ruíz de la Mota and Catalina Iñiguez de Escobar. De la Mota y Escobar, *Descripción geográfica*, 9–10.
21. De la Mota y Escobar, *Descripción geográfica*, 14.

22. De la Mota y Escobar, *Descripción geográfica*, 14–15.
23. De la Mota y Escobar, *Descripción geográfica*, presents an overview of late sixteenth- and early seventeenth-century Nueva Galicia.
24. De la Mota y Escobar, *Descripción geográfica*, 15.
25. Lister and Lister, *Chihuahua*, 28.
26. Lister and Lister, *Chihuahua*, 29–30.
27. Lister and Lister, *Chihuahua*, 32.
28. De la Mota y Escobar, *Descripción geográfica*, 121–23.
29. De la Mota y Escobar, *Descripción geográfica*, 122.
30. De la Mota y Escobar, *Descripción geográfica*, 123.
31. De la Mota y Escobar, *Descripción geográfica*, 122.
32. De la Mota y Escobar, *Descripción geográfica*, 124.
33. De la Mota y Escobar, *Descripción geográfica*, 124.
34. De la Mota y Escobar, *Descripción geográfica*, 124.
35. De la Mota y Escobar, *Descripción geográfica*, 139.
36. De la Mota y Escobar, *Descripción geográfica*, 140.
37. De la Mota y Escobar, *Descripción geográfica*, 145.
38. De la Mota y Escobar, *Descripción geográfica*, 146.
39. De la Mota y Escobar, *Descripción geográfica*, 139–55.
40. De la Mota y Escobar, *Descripción geográfica*, 174.
41. De la Mota y Escobar, *Descripción geográfica*, 175.
42. De la Mota y Escobar, *Descripción geográfica*, 176–77.
43. De la Mota y Escobar, *Descripción geográfica*, 177.
44. De la Mota y Escobar, *Descripción geográfica*, 179.
45. De la Mota y Escobar, *Descripción geográfica*, 179–80.
46. De la Mota y Escobar, *Descripción geográfica*, 182–83.
47. De la Mota y Escobar, *Descripción geográfica*, 184.
48. De la Mota y Escobar, *Descripción geográfica*, 180, 185.
49. De la Mota y Escobar, *Descripción geográfica*, 193.
50. De la Mota y Escobar, *Descripción geográfica*, 194.
51. De la Mota y Escobar, *Descripción geográfica*, 195.
52. De la Mota y Escobar, *Descripción geográfica*, 199–200.
53. De la Mota y Escobar, *Descripción geográfica*, 199–201.
54. Lister and Lister, *Chihuahua*, 37.
55. Alonso de Benavides, *Benavides' Memorial of 1630*, ed. Cyprian J. Lynch, trans. Peter P. Forrestal (Academy of American Franciscan History, 1954), 9–10.
56. Benavides, *Benavides' Memorial of 1630*, 14.

Chapter 4

1. Neumann, *Historia de las rebeliones*, 39.
2. Among missionaries mentioned by Father Neumann were "el padre Frantisek Retz, fue provincial del 4 de diciembre de 1718 al 21 de enero de 1720, y posteriormente, del 18 de julio de 1723 al 9 de junio de 1725; El padre Michelangelo

Tamburini, fue general de los jesuitas del 31 de enero de 1706 al 28 de febrero de 1730; El padre Gian Paolo Oliva fue general de los jesuitas del 31 de julio de 1664 al 26 de noviembre de 1681; Neumann fue superior de la Tarahumara de 1687 a 1690 y, posteriormente de 1702 a 1705, así como de 1711 a 1717; Neumann fue visitador de las misiones de la Tarahumara de 1696 a 1699, de 1705 a 1708 y entre 1711 y 1717. Después de mí, llegaron a esta tierra otros muchos misioneros, algunos de los cuales ya han muerto; a saber: el padre Adam Gilg; el padre Maximilian Amarel; el padre Johann Christoph Verdier; el padre Vaclav Eymer; el padre Villem lllingll; y hace poco, el 22 de febrero último, el padre Daniel Janusky. El padre Daniel Janusky, nació en 1662 en Wroclaw, Silesia, ingresó con los jesuitas en 1678. A fines de 1692 estuvo en la Tarahumara y en 1693 pasó a ocuparse de las misiones de Tubutama, Te6pari y Oposura en Sonora. Falleció en 1723. El padre Jirí Stanislav Hostinsky, nació en Valasské Klobouk, Moravia, en 1654, ingresó con los jesuitas en 1669." Neumann, *Historia de las rebeliones,* 46.

3. Neumann, *Historia de las rebeliones,* 18–19, n. 7.
4. Neumann, *Historia de las rebeliones,* 17–18, nn. 3–5.
5. Neumann, *Historia de las rebeliones,* 19–20.
6. Lister and Lister, *Chihuahua,* 30.
7. Neumann, *Historia de las rebeliones,* 44.
8. Neumann, *Historia de las rebeliones,* 24–26, 44–45; Lister and Lister, *Chihuahua,* 32.
9. Neumann, *Historia de las rebeliones,* 20–21.
10. Neumann, *Historia de las rebeliones,* 21–22.
11. Neumann, *Historia de las rebeliones,* 22.
12. Neumann, *Historia de las rebeliones,* 23.
13. Neumann, *Historia de las rebeliones,* 31, n. 8.
14. Neumann, *Historia de las rebeliones,* 31.
15. Neumann, *Historia de las rebeliones,* 33.
16. Joseph P. Sánchez, "Contested Ground: Indigenous Territoriality and European Sovereignty in the Early Centuries of European Discovery of and Claim to North America," *New Mexico Historical Review* 95, no. 2 (2020): 225.
17. Neumann, *Historia de las rebeliones,* 37–38, nn. 29 and 33.
18. Neumann, *Historia de las rebeliones,* 39.
19. Neumann, *Historia de las rebeliones,* 46.
20. Real de Santa Rosa, April 3, 1690, Carta del Padre Francisco de Selada, Archivo General de Indias, Seville, Spain, Patronato 236, microfilm roll 1, folder 1, frame 43b.
21. Real de Santa Rosa, April 3, 1690, Carta del Padre Francisco de Selada, frame 43b.
22. Real de Santa Rosa, April 3, 1690, Carta del Padre Francisco de Selada, frame 43b.
23. Neumann, *Historia de las rebeliones,* 47.

24. Neumann, *Historia de las rebeliones*, 48.
25. Neumann, *Historia de las rebeliones*, 49.
26. Neumann, *Historia de las rebeliones*, 50–51.
27. Neumann, *Historia de las rebeliones*, 51.
28. Neumann, *Historia de las rebeliones*, 52.
29. Neumann, *Historia de las rebeliones*, 52–53.
30. Neumann, *Historia de las rebeliones*, 54.
31. Neumann, *Historia de las rebeliones*, 54.
32. Neumann, *Historia de las rebeliones*, 55.
33. Neumann, *Historia de las rebeliones*, 56–57.
34. Neumann, *Historia de las rebeliones*, 58.
35. Neumann, *Historia de las rebeliones*, 58.
36. Conde de Galve to Juan Ignacio de Pardíñas, Mexico City, December 24, 1690, and January 3, 1691; Conde de Galve to General Retana, Mexico City, October 22, 1692, Archivo General de Indias, Patronato 236, microfilm roll 3, frames 133–42.

Chapter 5

1. Informe de estado de aquel Reyno, Nuevos descubrimientos de minerales que en el hay, y de excito de guerra, noticia de extranjeros por la parte del Norte de dicho Reino y providencia que ha dado a todo, de que reme testimonio. Don Juan Isidro de Pardíñas, Gobernador de la Nueva Vizcaya, A su Majestad, Parral, November 21, 1688. Recibido por mano Don Bernardino Pardíñas, su hermano, August 16, 1689, Archivo General de Indias (AGI), Audiencia de Guadalajara 29.
2. Pardíñas, Informe de estado de aquel Reyno.
3. Pardíñas, Informe de estado de aquel Reyno.
4. Carta signed by Capitán y Alcalde Mayor Francisco Ramírez de Casas Grandes, Archivo General de Indias, Patronato 236, microfilm roll 1, folder 1, frame 14b. See also Carta del Capitán Juan de la Fuente, Casas Grandes, March 16, 1690, Archivo General de Indias, Patronato 236, microfilm roll 1, folder 1, frame 31.
5. Francisco Ramírez to Governor Pardíñas, March 16, 1690, Archivo General de Indias, Patronato 236, microfilm roll 1, folder 1, frame 20b.
6. Letter from Father Diego Ortíz de Foronda to Governor Pardíñas, Yepómera, February 22, 1690, Archivo General de Indias, Patronato 236, microfilm roll 1, folder 1, frames 21a–21b.
7. Informes de Capitán Juan Fernández de la Fuente, Presidio de San Phelipe y Santiago de Janos, Capitán Francisco Pacheco Sevallos, Jesús de Baranuche y varios vecinos y mineros and don Juan de Escalante, teniente del Alcalde Mayor y Capitán, February 28, 1690, Real y Minas de Nuestra Rosario de Nacosari, Archivo General de Indias, Patronato 236, microfilm roll 1, folder 1, frames 23a–25b.
8. Informes de Capitán Juan Fernández de la Fuente et al.

9. Letter from Ramírez to Governor Pardíñas, Casas Grandes, March 10, 1690, Archivo General de Indias, Patronato 236, microfilm roll 1, folder 1, frame 15a.
10. Letter from Ramírez to Governor Juan Isidro de Pardíñas and General Marcos Fernandez de Castañeda, March 21, 1690, Santa Rosa, Archivo General de Indias, Patronato 236, microfilm roll 1, folder 1, frame 15b.
11. Governor Pardíñas, March 25, 1690, San Joseph de Parral, microfilm roll 1, folder 1, frames 15b–16a.
12. Governor Pardíñas, March 25, 1690.
13. Signed by Governor Pardíñas and other officers, March 25, 1690, San Joseph de Parral, Archivo General de Indias, Patronato 236, microfilm roll 1, folder 1, frames 16a–17a.
14. Francisco Ramírez to Governor Pardíñas, March 16, 1690, Archivo General de Indias, Patronato 236, microfilm roll 1, folder 1, frame 20a.
15. Neumann, *Historia de las rebeliones*, 59.
16. Neumann, *Historia de las rebeliones*, 59.
17. Neumann, *Historia de las rebeliones*, 59–60.
18. Neumann, *Historia de las rebeliones*, 60, n. 40.
19. Juan Ysidro de Pardíñas Villar de Francos Cavallero del horden de Santiago Governador y Capitán General de este Reino Y Provincias de la Nueva Viscaya por su Magestad; aviendose Conformado con los pareseres de la Junta que se hizo aier dos de este presente Mes en su Conformidad y para proveer de el Remedio para el Reparo, y defensa de la Sublevasion de las Naçiones Reveladas a la Real Corona, April 3, 1690, Archivo General de Indias, Patronato 23, folder 1, frame 39a, p. 67.
20. Governor Pardíñas introduces the series of testimonies in his communiqué to the viceroy in Carta de Juan Isidro Pardíñas Villadefrancos, Parral, April 1, 1693, Archivo General de Indias, Patronato 236, which includes additional reports to the viceroy dated March 30, 1693, in fols. 715–993.
21. Governor Pardíñas to the viceroy, February 5, 1693, Cuaderno 1, Guerra de Tarahumares, Pimas, Jobos, Conchos Tepeguanes and others, Real de Minas de San José de Parral, February 5, 1693, Archivo General de Indias, Patronato 236, fol. 715.
22. Among the testimonies is Testimonio de autos hechos por el General Juan de Retana en conformidad de horden del Señor Governador y Capitán General de este Reyno sobre la sublevazión de los taraumares.—Antes de aber en persona acudido Su Señoría. Y tocan al prinsipio de los autos de guerra de dicha nasión, Real y Minas de San José del Parral, March 30, 1693, Archivo General de Indias, Patronato 236, fols. 727–59. See also Nueva Viscaya, año de 1693, Testimonios de autos fechos por el General Juan de Retana sobre la vizita anual de los pueblos de la provincia de taraumares, en birtud de orden del Señor Governador y Capitán General Don Juan Isidro de Pardíñas Villardefrancos, Cavallareo de la Orden de Santiago, Real y Minas de San José del Parral, March 30, 1693, Archivo General de Indias, Patronato 236, fols. 803–61.

23. Included in Pardíñas's communique to the viceroy is Testimonio de los autos fechos por el Capitán Francisco Ramírez de Salazar y el Capitán Juan Fernández de la Fuente sobre el alzamiento de los conchos de la Sierra y tharaumares. 3—Este quaderno toca al prinsipio de la guerra de tharaumares formado en virtud de órdenes del Sr. Governador y Capitán General deste Reyno Don Juan Isidro de Pardíñas Villardefrancos, Cavallero de la Orden de Santiago. Quaderno que se acomula al bolumen de autos de tharaumares, Real y Minas de San José del Parral, March 30, 1693, Archivo General de Indias, Patronato 236, fols. 760–802.
24. Testimonio de los autos y demas delixenzias que el Señor Governador Y Capitan General de este Reino formo en la guerra y pazificazion de los Yndios de la nazion taraumara y sus aliados, Nueba Vizcaya año de 1693 = Cuaderno No. 1°, Guerra de Tharaumares, Pimas, Jobas, Conchos, Thepeguanes y otras; Testimonio de los autos fechos por el cappitán Francisco Ramírez de Salazar y el cappitán Juan Fernández de la Fuente sobre el alzamiento de los conchos de la Sierra y tharaumares, Real y Mines de San José de Parral, March 30, 1693, Archivo General de Indias. See also Francisco Ramírez de Salazar to Governor Pardíñas, Casas Grandes, March 10, 1690, Archivo General de Indias, Patronato 236, microfilm roll 1, fols. 760–892.
25. Juan Ysidro de Pardíñas Villar de Francos Cavallero, April 3, 1690.
26. Carta que acompaña à los seis ramos de autos fecha en el Parral del Gobernador y Capitan General de la Nueva Vizcaya Don Juan Ysidro de Pardíñas Villar de Francos dando cuenta de lo que ha mandado y obrado en la guerra que sostuvo contra los indios Taraumaraes y sus aliados que se habian levantado contra Dios y el Rey, April 20, 1693, Archivo General de Indias, Patronato Ramo 1, fols. 1–6.
27. Carta que acompaña à los seis ramos de autos, April 20, 1693, fol. 6.
28. Carta que acompaña à los seis ramos de autos, April 20, 1693, fol. 7.
29. Governor Pardíñas to the viceroy, May 30, 1690, as well as references to *noticias* received on March 30, 1690, Archivo General de Indias, Patronato 236, microfilm roll 1, folder 1, frame 18a.
30. Carta que acompaña à los seis ramos de autos, April 20, 1693, fol. 10.
31. Carta que acompaña à los seis ramos de autos, April 20, 1693, fols. 7 and 12.
32. Carta que acompaña à los seis ramos de autos, April 20, 1693, fol. 7.
33. Carta que acompaña à los seis ramos de autos, April 20, 1693, fol. 11.
34. Governor Diego Guajardo Fajardo was appointed on September 13, 1648. See Governor Don Luis Valdez al Rey Felipe IV, sobre la posición del gobernador Don Diego Guaxardo Faxardo, Durango, November 29, 1648, Archivo General de Indias, Audiencia de Guadalajara 29, fols. 48–53.
35. *Fiscal del Consejo de Indias*, Madrid, May 28, 1695, Archivo General de Indias, Patronato 236, microfilm roll 3, frames 197–202. This report presents a summary of the Indian rebellion from the Spanish perspective.
36. *Fiscal del Consejo de Indias*, Madrid, May 28, 1695.
37. *Fiscal del Consejo de Indias*, Madrid, May 28, 1695.
38. *Fiscal del Consejo de Indias*, Madrid, May 28, 1695.

39. Carta que acompaña à los seis ramos de autos, April 20, 1693, fol. 7.
40. Carta que acompaña à los seis ramos de autos, April 20, 1693, fol. 7.
41. Governor Pardíñas to the viceroy, May 30, 1690, frames 17b and 18a.
42. Carta que acompaña à los seis ramos de autos, April 20, 1693, fol. 11. In that document, Pardíñas recounts that "la sublebacion que la Nacion tharaumara hiço quitando la bida a sus Ministros misioneros destruyendo y quemando las Yglesias con sumiendo Reales de minas y haciendas."
43. Carta que acompaña à los seis ramos de autos, April 20, 1693, fol. 7.
44. *Fiscal del Consejo de Indias*, Madrid, May 28, 1695.
45. Carta del General don Marcos Fernández de Castañeda (to Governor Pardíñas), Papigochic, April 3, 1690, Archivo General de Indias, Patronato 236, microfilm roll 1, folder 1, frame 47a.
46. Governor Pardíñas to the viceroy, May 30, 1690, as well as references to *noticias* received on March 30, 1690, frame 18a.
47. *Fiscal del Consejo de Indias*, Madrid, May 28, 1695.

Chapter 6

1. See Retana's investigations regarding villages and missions visited in 1692: Archivo General de Indias, Patronato 236, microfilm roll 2, frames 521a–527b. Among the testimonies is Testimonio de autos hechos por el General Juan de Retana en conformidad de horden del Señor Governador y Capitán General de este Reyno sobre la sublevación de los taraumares.—Antes de aber en persona acudido Su Señoría. Y tocan al prinsipio de los autos de guerra de dicha nasión, Real y Minas de San José del Parral, March 30, 1693, Archivo General de Indias, Patronato 236, fols. 727–59. See also Nueva Viscaya, año de 1693, Testimonios de autos fechos por el General Juan de Retana sobre la visita anual de los pueblos de la provincia de taraumares, en birtud de orden del Señor Governador y Capitán General Don Juan Isidro de Pardíñas Villardefrancos, Cavallareo de la Orden de Santiago, Real y Minas de San José del Parral, March 30, 1693, Archivo General de Indias, Patronato 236, fols. 803–61.
2. Testimonies by Pato and Nicolas Garcia . . . En este pueblo en dicho Dia Mes Y año dichos actuando Como Jues receptor por no aber escribano publico ni Real Siendo Testigos Manuel Domingues Y Francisco de Cordoba = Don Marcos Fernández de Castañeda Jues receptor = Manuel Domingues = Francisco de Cordoba, [Yepache, December 20, 1691], Archivo General de Indias, Patronato 236, microfilm roll 2, folder 7, frame 549a.
3. Testimonies by Pato and Nicolas Garcia, frames 549b–550b.
4. Testimonies by Pato and Nicolas Garcia. As he could not write, don Joseph did not sign his sworn statement.
5. Testimonies by Pato and Nicolas Garcia, frame 551a. Not knowing how to write, Salvador swore his statement was true.
6. No Firmo por no saber escribir firmolo el Interpret con miso due acute como Juez Receptor por no amber escribano public . . . siendo testigos Manuel

Domingues y Francisco de Cordoba parese de cinquenta años dicho declarante y en su dicho se affirm a viendoslel dado a entender por dicho interprete, December 21, 1691, Archivo General de Indias, Patronato 236, microfilm roll 2, folder 7, frame 553a.

7. Testigo de Esteban de Quintina ante mi, Fernando de Ynojos, escribno de Guerra en el dicho Pueblo de Temaichi en seis del corrients, January 6, 1692, Archivo General de Indias, Patronato 236, microfilm roll 2, folder 7, frame 520.
8. En el Puesto y Pueblo de San Marcos de Pichachigui en ocho del corriente, signed by Retana and witnessed by Esteban de Quintana and Juan Hipoito de Echevarria and noted by Fernando de Ynojos, military scribe, Archivo General de Indias, Patronato 236, microfilm roll 2, folder 7, frame 522.
9. En el Puesto y Pueblo de San Marcos de Pichachigui, frames 521b–522.
10. Neumann, *Historia de las rebeliones*, 46–48.
11. Digo yo, el Capitan Joseph Lobo, Teniente de Justice Mayor de la Jurisdicción del Valle de Papigochi que certifíco en quanto puedo como el General don Gerónimo que lo es de la nación Tarahumara, December 1, 1691, Archivo General de Indias, Patronato 236, microfilm roll 2, folder 7, frame 529b.
12. En dicho Puesto de Pichachiqui Yo dicho Capitán Juan de Retana en dicho dia para efecto de aclarar lo que Refieren los dos papeles del Padre Joseph Nauman hise Compareser Ante mi al Governador de este puesto llamado Don Manuel a quien Resevi JuraMento que lo hiso por Dios nuestro Señor Y la señal de la cruz, January 8, 1692, Archivo General de Indias, Patronato 236, microfilm roll 2, folder 7, frames 521–22.
13. Geographically, Puerto de Moris de Pimas is presently located at 27° 57′—28° 23′ north latitude and 108° 24′–109° 05′ west longitude. "Municipio de Moris," Wikipedia, accessed December 1, 2023, https://es.wikipedia.org/wiki/Municipio_de_Moris.
14. Statement by the Alcalde Nicolás, January 6, 1692, Archivo General de Indias, Patronato 236, microfilm roll 2, folder 7, frame 522a.
15. En el Pueblo de Nuestra Señora del Populo de los Alamos en Nuebe del Corrientes [mes y año de 1692], Firme con los testigos de asistencia que lo fueron Esteban de Quintana y Juan Hipolito de Chavarria presentes = Juan de Retana, Archivo General de Indias, Patronato 236, microfilm roll 2, folder 7, frame 522.
16. Certificación en forma para que con ella en virtud del orden del Señor Governador y Capitan Genreal de este Reino haga requerimiento al Reverendo Padre Visitador Francisco María Piccolo provea de los padre ministros a dichos partidos en atención a tenerlos Consedidos, Archivo General de Indias, Patronato 236, microfilm roll 2, folder 7, frame 523b.
17. En el Pueblo de Jesús Carichiqui en trese del corriente yo, dacha Capitán Juan de Retana, estando juntos y congregates los natural deist pueblo, Archivo General de Indias, Patronato 236, microfilm roll 2, folder 7, frame 523a.
18. En dicho Pueblo de Jesús Carichiqui, yo Capitán Juan de Retan en atencion saber en mi companía el Reverendo Padre Rector Florencio de Alderete de la

Company de Jesús de los Partidos de Matachiqui, . . . pueblos Y partidos de Matachiqui, Yepomera Cocomorachi Arisiachi, Tomochi, Caguisorichi, Y tu tuaca, Con los Pueblos de Santo Thomas, Y pichachiqui, Para donde son los Padres Ministros nuebamente con Sedidos en atençion aber estado en todos los dichos partidos, Archivo General de Indias, Patronato 236, microfilm roll 2, folder 7, frame 523a.

19. Lo Firme Con los testigos de asistençia que Lo Fueron Esteban de Quintana y Juan Ypolito de Chavarria presentes = Juan de Retana = testigo Esteban de Quintana = testigo Juan Hipolito de Echavarriav = Ante mi Fernando de Ynojos escribano de guerra, January 19, 1692, Archivo General de Indias, Patronato 236, microfilm roll 2, folder 7, frames 524a–524b.
20. Lo Firme Con los testigos de asistençia, frames 524a–524b.
21. En el Puesto que llaman de la ConSepsion en Veinte Y quatro del corriente Yo dicho Capitán aViendo benido a este puesto halle que los naturales del se Componen de quarenta y dos Yndios a quienes hise Cargo dijesen por que Ministro Eran administrados Y a donde Yban a oir la Santa Misa quienes Respondieron aber algunos años que no tenian assistençia de Ministro por no benir, January 24, 1692, Archivo General de Indias, Patronato 236, microfilm roll 2, folder 7, frames 524b–527b.
22. Firme con los testigos de asistençia que lo fueron Esteban de Quintana Y Juan de Chavarria presentes = Juan de Retana = testigo Esteban de Quintana = testigo Juan Ypolito de Chavarria = Ante mi Fernando de Ynojos escribano de guerra, January 27, 1692, Archivo General de Indias, Patronato 236, microfilm roll 2, folder 7, frame 526a.
23. En el Puesto de las Cuebas en 26 del corriente . . . en el Pueblo de San Lorenzo . . . Y para sue asi conste lo fire con los testigos de mi asistencia sue lo son Esteban de Quintana y Juan de Chavarria presented—Juan de Retana, Archivo General de Indias, Patronato 236, microfilm roll 2, folder 7, frame 526b.
24. En el Pueblo de Santiago de Babonoiva en veinte y ocho del corriente, yo dicho capitán halle juntos y congregados a los naturals de este pueblo, Archivo General de Indias, Patronato 236, microfilm roll 2, folder 7, frame 526b.
25. Con los del Pueblo de Satebo por sir pestos dos pueblos como son fronteras dandole noticia del presidio quando tubieron noticia de entrada de enemigos, Archivo General de Indias, Patronato 236, microfilm roll 2, folder 7, frame 527a.
26. Con los del Pueblo de Satebo, frame 527a.
27. En esta Probinçia de Tharaumares, en cumplimiento del horden del Señor Governador, Y Capitán General, de este Reino y Respecto de las muchas eladas y niebes que nos han caido en las Sierras Y por esto hallarse toda la caballada estropeada Y maltratada por lo qual me hallo ajeno por agora de Pasar a la vista de los demas pueblos desta probinçia Si bien esta ejecutado en todo el horden de dicho Señor Governador resolvi el retirarme A mi presidio Y en otra ocasion acavar la visita de los pueblos que faltan asi lo provei mande y firme = Juan de

Retana = Ante mi Fernando de Ynojos escribano de guerra, Archivo General de Indias, Patronato 236, microfilm roll 2, folder 7, frame 527b.

28. Lo firmo = Don Juan Isidro de Pardíñas—En el Puesto de Santa Cruz, February 16, 1692, Archivo General de Indias, Patronato 236, microfilm roll 2, folder 7, frame 531a.
29. Lo firmo = Don Juan Isidro de Pardíñas, frame 531b.
30. Como esta mandado Y abisara por Carta a dicho Padre VisiTador Francisco Maria Piccolo despache Padre Misionero a administrar dicho partido expresandole el estado de obdiencia en sue lo hallare y lo tubiere quedandose con testimonio a la letra de la carta sue escribiere a dicho Padre Visitor sue ponder en los autos = y se le participa a dicho General don Marcos Fernández de Castañeda como el General don Juan Fernández de Tetana, February 16, 1692, Archivo General de Indias, Patronato 236, microfilm roll 2, folder 7, frames 531b–533b.
31. Agosto Dies Y nuebe de Mill Y Seiscientos y nobenta y un años = Su minor servitor y siervo de Vuestra Reverencia Joseph Neumann, Si no castigan al don Geronimo por el engaño de Osebac que resusito algun dia, Archivo General de Indias, Patronato 236, microfilm roll 2, folder 7, frame 235b.
32. Y si es cierta la muerte del dicho Ygnacio Osebac, En Parral en echo dias del mss de Septiembre de mil seiscientos y nobenta y un años, Archivo General de Indias, Patronato 236, microfilm roll 2, folder 7, frame 233a.
33. No dudo diran la verdad de lo se saben, February 16, 1692, Archivo General de Indias, Patronato 236, microfilm roll 2, folder 7, frame 536b; Don Geronimo para sue la remitiera al Parral sue bien conocida er para sue and an con embosses sue ere como Ana cabeza de un cabal de grande porque este declatante dice conocia muy bien a dice Ignociote due era demasiadamente alto y due se affirm en hello que estate encargado de la muerte del dicho . . . no firm po no saber escriber, February 16, 1692, Archivo General de Indias, Patronato 236, microfilm roll 2, folder 7, frame 552b.

Chapter 7

1. Puesto de Santa Clara Y octubre Dos de nobenta años Besa La Mano de Vuestra señoría Su mui Umilde Criado que Su Mano besa = Francisco Ramirez de Salasar = Señor Governador Y Capitán General Don Juan Ysidro de Pardíñas Villar de Francos, Archivo General de Indias, Patronato 236, microfilm roll 2, frames 229a–243.
2. Señor Sargento mayor Don Juan Ysidro de Pardíñas Villar de Francos Goverandor Y Capitan General de este Reino de la nueba Viscaya por Su Magestad Y espero en el zelo de Su señoria ber asi mismo Juntos Y Congregados en pueblo Como lo esta este los otros Tres Pueblos anexos a esta mision que son Nuestra Señora del Pilar de Bacahuriachic, el Santo Angelo de la guarda de Papigochic, y San Luis Gonzaga de Tahirachi y por Ser berdad lo Firme en esta mision de Jesus carichic en dies de octubre de mill Seiscientos Y nobenta = Francisco

Maria Piccolo de la Compañía de Jesus, Archivo General de Indias, Patronato 236, microfilm roll 2, frames 232a–234.

3. Plaza de Armas de Guerra Carichiqui probinçia de Tharaumares Y octubre onse de mill Seiscientos Y nobenta años = Don Juan Ysidro de Pardíñas Villar de Francos = Excelentísimo Señor Conde de Galve = este Traslado Fielmente Sacado es de la Carta que escrive El Señor Governador Y Capitán General al excelentísimo Señor Virrei de la nueba españa que de mandato de Su señoria lo saque para poner con los autos de guerra oi mes de octubre de mill Seiscientos Y nobenta años Don Luis de Valdes secretario de governacion Y guerra, Archivo General de Indias, Patronato 236, microfilm roll 2, frames 243–59.
4. En Santo Thomas en dies, y Siete dias de el mes de octubre de Mill Seiscientos Y Noventa años el Señor Sarxento mayor Don Juan ysidro de Pardíñas Villar de Francos Cavallero de el horden de Santiago Governador y Capitán General de este Reino de la nueba Vizcaya, Archivo General de Indias, Patronato 236, microfilm roll 2, folder 4, frame 244b.
5. Plaza de Armas de Guerra, frames 243–59.
6. A series of testimonies in which "Ladino" interpreters were used can be found in En el puesto de Santo Tomas en dies Y Siete Dias del mes de octubre de mill Seiscientos Y nobenta años el señor Sargento mayor Don Juan Ysidro de Pardíñas Villar de Francos Cavallero del Horden de Santiago Governador Y Capitán General de este Reino de la nueba Viscaia Dixo que por quanto Se alla en este Campo Un Yndio ladino en lengua Castellana, Archivo General de Indias, Patronato 236, microfilm roll 2, frames 243–59.
7. Firmo, y Ratifico siendole leido no Firmo por no Saver Firmolo Alonso Muños interprete de este Campo que se hallo presente no supo desir su edad es al pareser de sin quenta, y Sinco años y lo Firmo su Señoría= Don Juan Ysidro de Pardíñas Villar de Francos = Alonso Muños de Sepeda = Ante mi Don Luis de Valdes Secretario de Governacion y guerra, Archivo General de Indias, Patronato, microfilm roll 2, folder 4, frame 25. See also No Firmo por no Saver ni Andres Thomas interprete Firmolo el dicho Alonso Muños con su Señoría = Don Juan Ysidro de Pardíñas Villar de Francos = Alonso Muños de Sepeda = Ante mi Don Luis de Valdes Secretario de Governacion y guerra, En el Puesto de Santo Thomas en dies, y Siete dias de el mes de octubre de mill seissientos y Noventa años el Señor Sarxento mayor Don Juan Ysidro de Pardíñas Villar de Francos Cavallero de el horden de Santiago Governador Y Capitan General de este Reino de la Nueva Vizcaya por su Magestad hizo pareser ante si a Domingo Yndio prinsipal de el partido de Matachic ladino en lengua Castellana, Archivo General de Indias, Patronato 236, microfilm roll 2, frame 243.
8. Firmo, y Ratifico siendole leido no Firmo por no Saver Firmolo Alonso Muños, frame 245.
9. Firmo, y Ratifico siendole leido no Firmo por no Saver Firmolo Alonso Muños, frame 249a.

10. Firmo, y Ratifico siendole leido no Firmo por no Saver Firmolo Alonso Muños, frame 249a.
11. Firmo, y Ratifico siendole leido no Firmo por no Saver Firmolo Alonso Muños, frame 249a.
12. Neumann, *Historia de las rebeliones,* 141.
13. Neumann, *Historia de las rebeliones,* 142.
14. Neumann, *Historia de las rebeliones,* 142.
15. Neumann, *Historia de las rebeliones,* 143.
16. Neumann, *Historia de las rebeliones,* 143, n. 9.
17. Neumann, *Historia de las rebeliones,* 144.
18. Neumann, *Historia de las rebeliones,* 145.
19. Neumann, *Historia de las rebeliones,* 146.
20. Neumann, *Historia de las rebeliones,* 146.
21. Neumann, *Historia de las rebeliones,* 146.
22. Neumann, *Historia de las rebeliones,* 146–47.
23. Neumann, *Historia de las rebeliones,* 148.
24. Neumann, *Historia de las rebeliones,* 149.
25. Neumann, *Historia de las rebeliones,* 150.
26. Neumann, *Historia de las rebeliones,* 151.
27. Neumann, *Historia de las rebeliones,* 152–53.
28. Neumann, *Historia de las rebeliones,* 153.
29. Neumann, *Historia de las rebeliones,* 155.
30. Neumann, *Historia de las rebeliones,* 159.
31. Neumann, *Historia de las rebeliones,* 163.
32. David J. Weber, *Bárbaros: Spaniards and Their Savages in the Age of Enlightenment* (Yale University Press, 2005), 195–96.

BIBLIOGRAPHY

Archives

Archivo General de Indias, Seville, Spain
Archivo General de la Nación, Mexico City, Mexico
Archivo Histórico de Parral, Parral, Mexico
Archivo Histórico Nacional, Madrid, Spain
Biblioteca Nacional de Antropología e Historia, Mexico City, Mexico

Secondary Sources

Alegre, Francisco Javier. *Historia de la provincia de la Compañía de Jesús de Nueva España*. Edited by Ernest J. Burrus and Félix Zubillaga. New ed. 4 vols. Institutum Historicum, 1956–60.

Almada, Francisco R. *Diccionario de historia, geografía y biografía chihuahuenses*. Vol. 2. Ediciones del Azar, 1928.

Almada, Francisco R. *Diccionario de historia, geografía y biografía chihuahuenses*. Vol. 2. Ediciones del Azar, 2008.

Bancroft, Hubert Howe. *History of the North Mexican States and Texas*. 2 vols. Vols. 15 and 16 of *The Works of Hubert Howe Bancroft*. A. L. Bancroft, 1884.

Bandelier, Adolph Francis Alphonse. *A History of the Southwest: A Study of the Civilization and Conversion of the Indians in Southwestern United States and Northwestern Mexico from the Earliest Times to 1700*. Edited by Ernest J. Burrus. Biblioteca Apostolica Vaticana, 1969.

Bargalló, Modesto. *La minería y metalurgía en la América española durante la época colonial*. Fondo de Cultura Económica, 1955.

Benavides, Alonso de. *Benavides' Memorial of 1630*. Edited by Cyprian J. Lynch. Translated by Peter P. Forrestal. Academy of American Franciscan History, 1954.

Bolton, Herbert E., ed. *Spanish Exploration in the Southwest, 1542–1706*. Charles Scribner's Sons, 1916.

Burrus, Ernest J., and Félix Zubillaga, trans. and eds. *El noroeste de México: Documentos sobre las misiones Jesuíticas*. Universidad Nacional Autónoma de México, 1986.

Campbell, Ysla, ed. *El Contacto entre los españoles e indígenas en el norte de Nueva España*. Universidad Autónoma de Ciudad Juárez, 1992.

Cavo, Andrés. *Historia de México*. 1836. Reprint, Editorial Patria, 1949.

Cavo, Andrés. *Historia de México*. 1836. Reprint, Universidad Nacional Autónoma de México, 2013.

Chevalier, François. *Land and Society in Colonial Mexico: The Great Hacienda*. University of California Press, 1963.

Christelow, Allan. "Father Joseph Neumann, Jesuit Missionary to the Tarahumares." *Hispanic American Historical Review* 19, no. 4 (1939): 423–42.

de la Mota y Escobar, Alonso. *Descripción geográfica de los reinos de Nueva Galicia, Nueva Vizcaya y Nueva León*. Edited by Joaquín Ramírez Cabañas. Editorial Pedro Robredo, 1940.

Debo, Angie. *Geronimo: The Man, His Time, His Place*. University of Oklahoma Press, 1976.

Deeds, Susan M. *Defiance and Deference in Mexico's Colonial North: Indians Under Spanish Rule in Nueva Vizcaya*. University of Texas Press, 2003.

Deeds, Susan M. "Indigenous Responses to Mission Settlement in Nueva Vizcaya." In *The New Latin American Mission History*, edited by Erick Langer and Robert H. Jackson. University of Nebraska Press, 1995.

Dunne, Peter Masten, S.J. *Early Jesuit Missions in Tarahumara*. University of California Press, 1948.

González Rodríguez, Luis. *El noroeste novohispano en la época colonial*. Universidad Nacional Autónoma de México, 1993.

Lister, Florence C., and Robert H. Lister. *Chihuahua: Storehouse of Storms*. University of New Mexico Press, 1966.

McNeil, Kent. "The Louisiana Purchase: Indian and American Sovereignty in the Missouri Watershed." *Western Historical Quarterly* 50, no. 1 (2019): 17–42.

Mecham, J. Lloyd. *Francisco de Ibarra y la Nueva Vizcaya*. Translated by Víctor Meneguzzo Peruzzo. Universidad Juárez de Estado de Durango, 2005.

Naylor, Thomas H., and Charles W. Polzer, S.J., eds. *The Presidio and Militia on the Northern Frontier of New Spain: A Documentary History*. 2 vols. University of Arizona Press, 1986.

Neumann, Joseph P. *Historia de las rebeliones en la sierra tarahumara (1626–1724)*. Edited by Luis González Rodríguez. Translated by Joaquín Díaz Anchondo and Luis González Rodríguez. Colección Centenario 8. Editorial Camino, 1991.

Pacheco Rojas, José de la Cruz. *Milenarismo tepehuán: Mesianismo y resistencia indígena en el norte novohispano*. Siglo XXI Editores, 2008.

Pérez de Ribas, Andrés. *History of the Triumphs of Our Holy Faith Among the Most Barbarous and Fierce Peoples of the New World*. Translated by Daniel T. Reff, Maureen Ahern, and Richard Danford. University of Arizona Press, 1999.

Polzer, Charles W, S.J. *Rules and Precepts of the Jesuit Missions of Northwestern New Spain*. University of Arizona Press, 1976.

Powell, Philip Wayne. *Soldiers, Indians and Silver: The Northward Advance of New Spain, 1550–1600*. University of California Press, 1969.

Recopilación de las Leyes de los Reinos de las Indias. Vol. 2. Ediciones Cultura Hispánica, 1973.

Salmón, Roberto Mario. *Indian Revolts in Northern New Spain: A Synthesis of Resistance, 1680–1786*. University Press of America, 1991.

Salmón, Roberto Mario. "Tarahumara Resistance to Mission Congregation in Northern New Spain, 1580–1710." *Ethnohistory* 24, no. 4 (1977): 379–93.

Sánchez, Joseph P. *El Camino Real de California: From Ancient Pathways to Modern Byways*. University of New Mexico Press, 2019.

Sánchez, Joseph P. "Contested Ground: Indigenous Territoriality and European Sovereignty in the Early Centuries of European Discovery of and Claim to North America." *New Mexico Historical Review* 95, no. 2 (2020): 213–36.

Sánchez, Joseph P. "Indigenous Territoriality and European Sovereignty in the Early Centuries of European Discovery of and Claim to North America." *New Mexico Historical Review* 95, no. 2 (Spring 2020): 213–38.

Sánchez, Joseph P. "Old Heat and New Light on Spanish Diplomacy Regarding the Louisiana Purchase and the Defense of New Mexico, 1762–1819." *Louisiana History* 64, no. 1 (Winter 2023): 5–43.

Sánchez, Joseph P. *Pueblos, Plains, and Province: New Mexico in the Seventeenth Century*. University Press of Colorado, 2021.

Sánchez, Joseph P., and Bruce A. Erickson, comps. *From Mexico City to Santa Fe: A Historical Guide to Geographic Place Names Along El Camino Real de Tierra Adentro*. Rio Grande Press, 2011.

Sánchez, Joseph P., and Bruce A. Erickson, comps. *From Saltillo, Mexico, to San Antonio and East Texas: An Historical Guide to El Camino Real de Tierra Afuera and El Camino Real de lo Tejas During the Spanish Colonial Period*. Rio Grande Press, 2016.

Sheridan, Thomas E., and Thomas H. Naylor. *Rarámuri: A Tarahumara Colonial Chronicle, 1607–1791*. Northland Press, 1979.

Wauer, Roland H., and David H. Riskind, eds. *Transactions of the Symposium on the Biological Resources of the Chihuahuan Desert Region: United States and Mexico*. Transactions and Precedence's Series 3. U.S. Department of the Interior, National Park Service, 1977.

Weber, David J. *Bárbaros: Spaniards and Their Savages in the Age of Enlightenment*. Yale University Press, 2005.

Further Reading

Aboites, Luis. *Breve historia de Chihuahua*. Fideicomiso Historia de las Américas, El Colegio de México / Fondo de Cultura Económica, 1994.

Aboites Aguilar, Luis. "Nómadas y sedentarios en el norte de México: Elementos para una periodización." In *Nómadas y sedentarios en el norte de México: Homenaje a Beatriz Braniff*, edited by Marie-Areti Hers et al. Universidad Nacional Autónoma de México, 2000.

Acuña Delgado, Ángel. *Etnología de la carrera de bola y ariweta rarámuris*. Centro de Investigaciones y Estudios Superiores en Antropología Social, 2006.

Acuña Delgado, Ángel. "Matachines tarahumaras: Reinventando la tradición." *Revista de Antropología Experimental*, no. 8 (2008): 29–39.

Alegre, Francisco Javier. *Historia de la Compañía de Jesús en Nueva-España*. Vol. 3. Edited by Carlos María de Bustamante. J. M. Lara, 1842.

Álvarez, Salvador. "Agricultores de paz y cazadores-recolectores de guerra: Los tobosos de la cuenca del río Conchos en la Nueva Vizcaya." In *Nómadas y sedentarios en el norte de México: Homenaje a Beatriz Braniff*, edited by Marie-Areti Hers et al. Universidad Nacional Autónoma de México, 2000.

Álvarez, Salvador. "El pueblo de indios en la frontera septentrional novohispana." *Relaciones* 24, no. 95 (2003): 115–64.

Arrieta, Olivia. "Religion and Ritual Among the Tarahumara Indians of Northern Mexico: Maintenance of Cultural Autonomy Through Resistance and Transformation of Colonizing Symbols." *Wicazo Sa Review* 8, no. 2 (Autumn 1992): 11–23.

Artaud, Antonin. *Viaje al país de los tarahumaras*. Edited by Luis Mario Schneider. Secretaría de Educación Público, 1975.

Bandelier, Adolph Francis Alphonse. *A History of the Southwest: A Study of the Civilization and Conversion of the Indians in Southwestern United States and Northwestern Mexico from the Earliest Times to 1700*. 2 vols. New ed. University of New Mexico Press, 1984.

Bargellini, Clara. "Arquitectura jesuita en la Tarahumara: ¿centro o periferia?" In *Órdenes religiosas entre América y Asia: Ideas para una historia misionera de los espacios coloniales*, edited by Elisabetta Corsi. El Colegio de México, 2008.

Bargellini, Clara. "At the Center, on the Frontier: The Jesuit Tarahumara Missions of New Spain." In *Time and Place: The Geohistory of Art*, edited by Thomas DaCosta Kaufmann and Elizabeth Pilliod. Ashgate, 2005.

Basauri, Carlos. *La población indígena de México*. Vol. 1. Instituto Nacional Indigenista, 1990.

Beals, Ralph L. *The Comparative Ethnology of Northern Mexico Before 1750*. University of California Press, 1932.

Bennet, Wendell C., and Robert M. Zingg. *The Tarahumara: An Indian Tribe of Northern Mexico*. Rio Grande Press, 1976.

Bennet, Wendell C., and Robert M. Zingg. *Los tarahumaras: Una tribu india del norte de México*. Instituto Nacional Indigenista, 1978.

Bernabéu Albert, Salvador. "La invención del Gran Norte ignaciano: La historiografía sobre la Compañía de Jesús entre dos centenarios (1992–2006)." In *El gran norte mexicano: Indios, misioneros y pobladores entre el mito y la historia*, edited by Salvador Bernabéu Albert. Consejo Superior de Investigaciones Científicas, 2009.

Bernabéu Albert, Salvador, ed. *El septentrión novohispano: Ecohistoria, sociedades e imágenes de frontera*. Consejo Superior de Investigaciones Científicas, 2000.

Binková, Simona. "El vocabulario tarahumar de Mateo Steffel como reflejo de su experiencia novohispana." *Ibero-Americana Pragensia* 26 (1992): 263–72.

Bonfiglioli, Carlo. *Fariseos y matachines en la Sierra Tarahumara: Entre la pasión de Cristo, la transgresión cómico-sexual y las danzas de conquista*. Instituto Nacional Indigenista, 1995.

Bonfiglioli, Carlo. "Fariseos y matachines tarahumaras: Simbolismo y apropiación simbólica de dos danzas de conquista." In *El noroeste de México: Sus culturas étnicas; Seminario de etnografía "Fernando Cámara Barbachano,"* edited by Donaciano Gutiérrez and Josefina Gutiérrez Tripp. Instituto Nacional de Antropología e Historia, 1991.

Bonfiglioli, Carlo, et al., eds. *Las vías del noroeste I: Una macrorregión indígena americana* Universidad Nacional Autónoma de México, 2006.

Bonfiglioli, Carlo, et al., eds. *Las vías del noroeste II: Propuesta para una perspectiva sistémica e indisciplinaria*. Universidad Nacional Autónoma de México, 2008.

Bonfiglioli, Carlo, et al., eds. *Las vías del noroeste III: Genealogías, transversalidades y convergencias*. Universidad Nacional Autónoma de México, 2011.

Borges Morán, Pedro. *El envío de misioneros a América durante la época española*. Universidad Pontificia, 1977.

Braniff C., Beatriz, ed. *La Gran Chichimeca: El lugar de las rocas secas*. Consejo Nacional para la Cultura y las Artes, 2001.

Burrus, Ernest J. "Francesco Maria Piccolo (1654–1729): Pioneer of Lower California in Light of Roman Archives." *Hispanic American Historical Review* 35, no. 1 (February 1955): 61–76.

Burrus, Ernest J. *Misiones norteñas mexicanas de la Compañía de Jesús, 1751–1757*. Antigua Librería Robredo de J. Porrúa, 1963.

Burrus, Ernest J., and Félix Zubillaga, eds. *Misiones mexicanas de la Compañía de Jesús, 1618–1745: Cartas e informes conservados de la "Colección Mateu."* J. Porrúa Turanzas, 1982.

Cajas Castro, Juan. *La Sierra Tarahumara o los desvelos de la modernidad en México*. Consejo Nacional para la Cultura y las Artes, 1992.

Castellanos Lira, Arturo. *Nueva crónica de un país bárbaro: Diagnóstico crítico de Chihuahua*. Costa-Amic Editors, 1974.

Cramaussel, Chantal. "De cómo los españoles clasificaban a los indios: Naciones y encomiendas en le Nueva Vizcaya central." In *Nómadas y sedentarios en el norte de México: Homenaje a Beatriz Braniff*, edited by Marie-Areti Hers et al. Universidad Nacional Autónoma de México, 2000.

Cramaussel, Chantal. "Un desconocimiento peligroso: La Nueva Vizcaya en la cartografía y los grandes textos europeos de los siglos XVI y XVII." *Relaciones* 75, no. 19 (Summer 1998): 174–211.

Cramaussel, Chantal. "Evolución de las formas de dominio en el espacio colonial: Las haciendas de la región de Parral." In *Actas del Segundo Congreso de Historia Regional Comparada 1990*, edited by Ricardo León García. Universidad Autónoma de Ciudad Juárez, 1991.

Cramaussel, Chantal. *Poblar la frontera: La Provincia de Santa Bárbara en Nueva Vizcaya durante los siglos XVI y XVII*. El Colegio de Michoacán, 2006.

Cuello, José. "The Persistence of Indian Slavery and Encomienda in the Northeast of Colonial Mexico, 1577–1723." *Journal of Social History* 21, no. 4 (1988): 683–700.

De Velasco Rivero, Pedro J. *Danzar o morir: Religión y resistencia a la dominación en la cultura tarahumara*. ITESO, Universidad Jesuita de Guadalajara, 2006.

Decorme, Gerard. *La obra de los jesuítas mexicanos durante la época colonial, 1572–1767*. 2 vols. Antigua Librería Robredo de José Porrúa e Hijos, 1941.

Deeds, Susan M. "Cómo historiar con poca historia y menos arqueología: Clasificación de los acaxes, xiximes, tepehuanes, tarahumaras y conchos." In *Nómadas y sedentarios en el norte de México: Homenaje a Beatriz Braniff*, edited by Marie-Areti Hers et al. Universidad Nacional Autónoma de México, 2000.

Deeds, Susan M. "First Generation Rebellions in Seventeenth-Century Nueva Vizcaya." In *Native Resistance and the Pax Colonial in New Spain*, edited by Susan Schroeder. University of Nebraska Press, 1998.

Deeds, Susan M. "Mission Villages and Agrarian Patterns in a Nueva Vizcaya Heartland, 1600–1750." *Journal of the Southwest* 33, no. 3 (Autumn 1991): 345–65.

Deeds, Susan M. "Las rebeliones de los tepehuanes y tarahumaras durante el siglo XVII en la Nueva Vizcaya." In *El Contacto entre los españoles e indígenas en el norte de la Nueva España*, edited by Ysla Campbell. Universidad Autónoma de Ciudad Juárez, 1992.

Deeds, Susan M. "Las rebeliones tarahumaras del siglo XVII." *Dos estudios de historia regional colonial: Cuadernos de trabajo* 7 (Fall 1992): 7–13.

Deeds, Susan M. "Resistencia indígena y vida cotidiana en la Nueva Vizcaya: Trastornos y cambios étnico-culturales en la época colonial." In *Identidad y cultura en la Sierra Tarahumara*, edited by Claudia Molinari and Eugeni Porras. Instituto Nacional de Antropología e Historia / Congreso del Gobierno del Estado de Chihuahua, 2001.

Deeds, Susan M. "Rural Work in Nueva Vizcaya: Forms of Labor Coercion on the Periphery." *Hispanic American Historical Review* 69, no. 3 (August 1989): 425–49.

Deeds, Susan M. "Subverting the Social Order: Gender, Power, and Magic in Nueva Vizcaya." In *Choice, Persuasion, and Coercion: Social Control on Spain's North American Frontiers*, edited by Jesús F. de la Teja and Ross Frank. University of New Mexico Press, 2005.

Del Valle, Ivonne. *Escribiendo desde los márgenes: Colonialismo y jesuítas en el siglo XVIII*. Siglo XXI Editores, 2009.

Dunne, Peter Masten. *Pioneer Jesuits in Northern Mexico*. University of California Press, 1944.

Dunne, Peter Masten. "Tomás de Guadalajara: Missionary of the Tarahumares." *Mid-America* 12 (October 1941): 272–87.

Estrada Fernández, Zarina, and Aarón Grajeda Bustamante. "¿'Naciones' de enemigos? La identificación de los indios rebeldes en la Nueva Vizcaya (siglo XVII)." In *El gran norte mexicano: Indios, misioneros y pobladores entre el mito y la historia*, edited by Salvador Bernabéu Albert. Consejo Superior de Investigaciones Científicas, 2009.

Estrada Fernández, Zarina, and Aarón Grajeda Bustamante. "Las obras sobre tarahumara de Thomás de Guadalaxara y Matthäus Steffel: Un acercamiento interdisciplinario." In *Lenguas, estructuras y hablantes: Estudios en homenaje a Thomas C. Smith Stark*. El Colegio de México, 2014.

Félix Gastélum, José Rómulo, and Raquel Padilla Ramos, eds. *Misiones del noroeste de México: Origen y destino 2005*. Consejo Nacional para la Cultura y las Artes, 2007.

Fontana, Bernard L. *Tarahumara, Where Night Is the Day of the Moon*. Northland Press, 1979.

Frost, Elsa Cecilia. "La crónica general jesuita." *Novahispania* 4 (1998): 183–93.

Gerhard, Peter. *The North Frontier of New Spain*. University of Oklahoma Press, 1993.

González de Cossío, Francisco. *Crónicas de la Compañía de Jesús en la Nueva España*. Universidad Nacional Autónoma de México, 1957.

González Rodríguez, Luis. "Las barrancas tarahumaras." *Estudios de historia novohispana* 5 (1974): 111–41.

González Rodríguez, Luis. "La evangelización en la Tarahumara (1604–1767)." In *El noroeste de México: Sus culturas étnicas; Seminario de etnografía "Fernando Cámara Barbachano,"* edited by Donaciano Gutiérrez and Josefina Gutiérrez Tripp. Instituto Nacional de Antropología e Historia, 1991.

González Rodríguez, Luis. "Las guerrillas de resistencia étnica en el noroeste (1690): Un análisis de la documentación oficial." In *Organización y liderazgo en los movimientos populares novohispanos*, edited by Felipe Castro Gutiérrez, Virginia Guedea, and José Luis Mirafuentes Galván. Universidad Nacional Autónoma de México, 1992.

González Rodríguez, Luis. "Iván Ratkaj, de la nobleza croata, misionero jesuita e historiador de la Tarahumara (1647–1683)." In "Relación de las misiones de la Tarahumara y descripción de la nación tarahumara y de su tierra," special issue, *Anales de antropología* 31 (1994): 203–44.

González Rodríguez, Luis. "Joseph Neumann, 1648–1732: Historiador y etnógrafo de la Tarahumara." *Ibero-Americana Pragensia* 20 (1986): 141–58.

González Rodríguez, Luis. *Tarahumara: La sierra y el hombre*. Fondo de Cultura Económica, 1982.

González Rodríguez, Luis. "Testimonios sobre la destrucción de las misiones tarahumaras y pimas en 1690." *Estudios de historia novohispana* 10, no. 10 (January 1991): 189–235.

González Rodríguez, Luis. "Thomas de Guadalaxara (1648–1720), misionero de la Tarahumara, historiador, lingüista y pacificador." *Estudios de historia novohispana* 15 (1995): 9–34.

González Rodríguez, Luis, and María Del Carmen Anzures y Bolaños. "Diccionario de misioneros de la Tarahumara, Chihuahua, México (1593–1767)." In *Un reino en la frontera: Las misiones jesuitas en la América colonial*, edited by Sandra Negro and Manuel M. Marzal. Fondo Editorial de la Pontificia Universidad Católica del Perú, 1999.

González Sobrino, Blanca Zoila, ed. *Entre tarahumaras, coras y huicholes: Algunos aspectos sobre la "locura."* Universidad Nacional Autónoma de México, 2012.

Gradie, Charlotte M. *The Tepehuan Revolt: Militarism, Evangelism, and Colonialism in Seventeenth-Century Nueva Vizcaya.* University of Utah Press, 2000.

Graham, Martha. *Mobile Farmers: An Ethnoarchaeological Approach to Settlement Organization Among the Rarámuri of Northwestern Mexico.* International Monographs in Prehistory, 1994.

Granados Pérez, Victoria. *Los costos de la modernidad: Transformaciones económicas en un pueblo rarámuri.* Instituto Chihuahuaense de la Cultura, 2006.

Griffen, William B. *Culture Change and Shifting Populations in Central Northern Mexico.* University of Arizona Press, 1969.

Griffen, William B. *Indian Assimilation in the Franciscan Area of Nueva Vizcaya.* University of Arizona Press, 1979.

Guadalajara, Tomás de. *Historia de la tercera rebelión tarahumara.* Edited by Roberto Ramos. Sociedad Chihuahuense de Estudios Históricos, 1950.

Guevara S., Arturo. "Algunos aspectos de la aculturación de los grupos conchos del centro del estado de Chihuahua." In *Actas del Segundo Congreso de Historia Regional Comparada 1990,* edited by Ricardo León García. Universidad Autónoma de Ciudad Juárez, 1991.

Hackett, Charles Wilson, ed. *Historical Documents Relating to New Mexico, Nueva Vizcaya, and Approaches Thereto, to 1773.* Vol. 2. Carnegie Institution, 1926.

Hausberger, Bernd. "La vida cotidiana de los misioneros jesuitas en el noroeste novohispano." *Estudios de historia novohispana* 17 (1997): 63–106.

Hausberger, Bernd. "La vida en el noroeste: Misiones jesuitas, pueblos y reales de minas." In *Historia de la vida cotidiana en México,* vol. 1, *Mesoamérica y los ámbitos indígenas de la Nueva España,* edited by Pablo Escalante Gonzalbo. El Colegio de México, 2004.

Hernández Palomo, José Jesús, and Rodrigo Moreno Jeria, eds. *La misión y los jesuitas en la América española, 1566–1767: Cambios y permanencias.* Consejo Superior de Investigaciones Científicas, 2005.

Hillerkuss Finn, Thomas. "Jesuitas y aculturación de los tarahumaras del siglo XVII." In *Los jesuitas en el norte de Nueva España: Sus contribuciones a la educación y el sistema misional,* edited by José de la Cruz Pacheco Rojas. Universidad Juárez del Estado de Durango, 2004.

Hope, Margarita. "Balance crítico de las investigaciones sobre la Sierra Tarahumara en la ENAH Chihuahua." In *La investigación antropológica y la formación profesional en el norte de México,* edited by Mónica Sofía Iturbide Robles. Escuela de Antropología e Historia del Norte de México, 2013.

Hope, Margarita. "Los olvidados: Algunas reflexiones sobre la etnografía de los grupos indígenas minoritarios de Chihuahua y Sonora." In *Antropología en las orillas,* edited by Victoria Novelo and Juan Luis Sariego. Universidad Intercultural de Chiapas, 2011.

Hu-DeHart, Evelyn. *Missionaries, Miners, and Indians: Spanish Contact with the Yaqui Nation of Northwestern New Spain, 1533–1820.* University of Arizona Press, 1981.

Huerta, María Teresa, and Patricia Palacios, eds. *Rebeliones indígenas de la época colonial.* Instituto Nacional de Antropología e Historia, 1976.

Huerta Preciado, María Teresa. *Rebeliones indígenas en el noroeste de México en le época colonial.* Universidad Nacional Autónoma de México, 1966.

Humboldt, Alejandro de. *Ensayo político sobre el Reino de la Nueva España.* Edited by Juan A. Ortega y Medina. Porrúa, 1966.

Illades, Lilián. "Labor misionera y herencia cultural y política de los jesuitas centroeuropeos en la provincia de la Alta Tarahumara de México." In *Emigración centroeuropea a América Latina II,* edited by Josef Opatrny. Universidad Carolina de Praga / Editorial Karolinum, 2003.

Jáuregui, Jesús. "Del ayuno al hartazgo: Guerra, sacrificio humano y canibalismo en la Sierra madre Occidental." In *Seminario: La religión y los jesuitas en el noroeste novohispano,* edited by José Carlos Zazueta Manjarrez. Memoria 5. El Colegio de Sinaloa, 2012.

Irigoyen Rascón, Fructuoso, and Jesús Manuel Palma Batista. *Rarajípari: La carrera de la bola tarahumara.* Centro Librero La Prensa, 1994.

Jiménez, Alfredo. *El gran norte de México: Una frontera imperial en la Nueva España, 1540–1820.* Tébar, 2006.

Jones, Oakah L., Jr. *Nueva Vizcaya: Heartland of the Spanish Frontier.* University of New Mexico Press, 1988.

Jordán, Fernando. *Crónica de un país bárbaro.* La Prensa, 1981.

Kašpar, Oldřich. *Los jesuitas checos en la Nueva España, 1678–1767.* Universidad Iberoamericana, 1991.

Kennedy, John G. *Tarahumara of the Sierra Madre: Beer, Ecology, and Social Organization.* AHM Publishing Corporation, 1978.

Křížová, Markéta. "Buscar a Dios en el fin del mundo: Los jesuitas de Provincia de Bohemia en México, siglos XVII y XVIII." In *Las relaciones checo-mexicanas,* edited by Josef Opatrny. Universidad Carolina de Praga / Editorial Karolinum, 2011.

Křížová, Markéta. *La ciudad ideal en el desierto: Proyectos misionales de la Compañía de Jesús y la Iglesia Morava en la América colonial.* Universidad Carolina de Praga / Editorial Karolinum, 2004.

León García, Ricardo. "Nuevas reflexiones en torno a las misiones jesuitas en la tarahumara." In *Los jesuitas en el norte de Nueva España: Sus contribuciones a la educación y el sistema misional,* edited by José de la Cruz Pacheco Rojas. Universidad Juárez del Estado de Durango, 2004.

Levi, Jerome M. "The Bow and the Blanket: Religion, Identity and Resistance in Raramuri Material Culture." *Journal of Anthropological Research* 54, no. 3 (Autumn 1998): 299–324.

Lumholtz, Carl. *Unknown Mexico: A Record of Five Year's Exploration Among the Tribes of the Western Sierra Madre; in the Tierra Caliente of Tepic and Jalisco; and Among the Tarascos of Michoacán*. Río Grande Press, 1973.

Magallanes Castañeda, Irma Leticia. "Desafíos misioneros jesuíticos en la Tepehuana y la Tarahumara: Un balance historiográfico." In *El gran norte mexicano: Indios, misioneros y pobladores entre el mito y la historia*, edited by Salvador Bernabéu Albert. Consejo Superior de Investigaciones Científicas, 2009.

Magriñá, Laura, et al. *Misiones en el noroeste de México*. Fondo Regional para la Cultura y las Artes del Noroeste, 2003.

Mancera-Valencia, Federico J. "Historia ambiental de la Sierra Tarahumara." In *Chihuahua Hoy 2004: Visiones de su historia, economía, política y cultura*, edited by Víctor Orozco. Universidad Autónoma de Ciudad Juárez, 2004.

"Maps of the Jesuit Mission in Spanish America, 18th Century (Archives of the Society of Jesus, Rome, *Hist. Soc. 150, I*)." *Imago Mundi* 15 (1960): 114–18.

Mares Trías, Albino. *Ralámuli Nu'tugala Go'ame: Comida de los tarahumaras; En tarahumara del oeste, de Bacusínare, Mpio. de Guazapares, Chihuahua, y en español*. 1982. Reprint, Consejo Nacional para la Cultura y las Artes, 1999.

Marini, Mario, and Salvatore Schembri. *Misioneros italianos en México*. El Consejo Episcopal Latinoamericano y Caribeño, 1989.

Márquez Terrazas, Zacarías, ed. *El informe Medrano: La Nueva Vizcaya en el siglo XVII*. Universidad Autónoma de Ciudad Juárez, 2005.

Márquez Terrazas, Zacarías. *Misiones de Chihuahua, siglos XVII y XVIII*. Consejo Nacional para la Cultura y las Artes, 2008.

Márquez Terrazas, Zacarías. *Satevó: Período colonial*. Gobierno del Estado de Chihuahua, 1990.

Martínez, John J. *Not Counting the Cost: Jesuit Missionaries in Colonial Mexico—a Story of Struggle, Commitment, and Sacrifice*. Loyola Press, 2001.

Mathes, W. Michael. "Jesuit Chroniclers and Chronicles of Northwestern Spain." In *Jesuit Encounters in the New World: Jesuit Chroniclers, Geographers, Educators and Missionaries in the Americas, 1549–1767*, edited by Joseph A. Gagliano and Charles E. Ronan. Institutum Historicum, 1997.

Mecham, J. Lloyd. *Francisco de Ibarra and Nueva Vizcaya*. Duke University Press, 1927.

Merrill, William L. "Conversion and Colonialism in Northern Mexico: The Tarahumara Response to the Jesuit Mission Program, 1601–1767." In *Conversion to Christianity: Historical and Anthropological Perspectives on a Great Transformation*, edited by Robert W. Hefner. University of California Press, 1993.

Merrill, William L. "La identidad ralámuli, una perspectiva histórica." In *Identidad y cultura en la Sierra Tarahumara*, edited by Claudia Molinari and Eugeni Porras. Instituto Nacional de Antropología e Historia, 2001.

Merrill, William L. "Indigenous Societies, Missions, and the Colonial System in Northern New Spain." In *The Art of the Missions of Northern New Spain, 1600–*

1821, edited by Clara Bargellini and Michael K. Komanecky. Mandato Antiguo Colegio de San Ildefonso, 2009.

Merrill, William L. "La obra lingüística del padre Matthäu Steffel S.J." In *Desde los confines de los imperios ibéricos: Los jesuitas de habla alemana en las misiones americanas*, edited by Karl Kohut and María Cristina Torales Pacheco. Vervuert, 2007.

Merrill, William L. *Rarámuri Souls: Knowledge and Social Process in Northern Mexico*. Smithsonian Institution, 1988.

Merrill, William L. "Tarahumara Social Organization, Political Organization, and Religion." In *Handbook of North American Indians*, vol. 10. Smithsonian Institution, 1983.

Mirafuentes Galván, José Luis, ed., *Movimientos de resistencia y rebeliones indígenas en el norte de México (1680–1821): Guía documental*. Vol. 1. Universidad Nacional Autónoma de México, 1989.

Mirafuentes Galván, José Luis, ed. *Movimientos de resistencia y rebeliones indígenas en el norte de México (1680–1821): Guía documental*. Vol. 2. Universidad Nacional Autónoma de México, 1993.

Molinari, Claudia, and Eugeni Porras, eds. *Identidad y cultura en la Sierra Tarahumara*. Instituto Nacional de Antropología e Historia, 2001.

Montiel Contreras, Carlos Urani. "Santa Rosa de Lima: Patrona de pueblos en la Sierra Tarahumara." In *Chihuahua Hoy 2013: Visiones de su historia, economía, política y cultura*, vol. 11, edited by Víctor Orozco. Universidad Autónoma de Ciudad Juárez, 2013.

Morales, Martín. "La respiración de ausentes: Itinerario por la escritura jesuítica." In *Saberes de la conversión: Jesuitas, indígenas e imperios coloniales en las fronteras de la cristiandad*, edited by Guillermo Wilde. Editorial SB, 2011.

Navarro García, Luis. *Sonora y Sinaloa en el siglo XVII*. Escuela de Estudios Hispano-Americanos, 1967.

Noyola, Antonio. *En busca del jícuri: El peyote en la Tarahumara*. Consejo Nacional para la Cultura y las Artes, 2008.

Obregón, Baltasar de. *Historia de los descubrimientos antiguos y nuevos de la Nueva España, escrita por el conquistador Baltasar de Obregón, año de 1584*. Secretaria de Educación Pública, 1924.

Odložilík, Otakar. "Czech Missionaries in New Spain." *Hispanic American Historical Review* 25, no. 4 (November 1945): 428–54.

Olavarría, María Eugenia, and Isabel Martínez, eds. *Estudios sobre parentesco rarámuri y ranchero en el norte de México*. Universidad Nacional Autónoma de México / Miguel Ángel Porrúa, 2012.

Ortega Noriega, Sergio. *Un ensayo de historia regional: El noroeste de México, 1530–1880*. Universidad Nacional Autónoma de México, 1993.

Ortega Noriega, Sergio. "La penetración española en el noroeste de México, del siglo XVI al XVIII." In *El noroeste de México: Sus culturas étnicas; Seminario de etnografía "Fernando Cámara Barbachano,"* edited by Donaciano Gutiérrez and Josefina Gutiérrez Tripp. Instituto Nacional de Antropología e Historia, 1991.

Ortelli, Sara. "Guerra y pacificación en las fronteras hispanoamericanas coloniales: La provincia de Nueva Vizcaya en tiempos de los Borbones." In *El gran norte mexicano: Indios, misioneros y pobladores entre el mito y la historia,* edited by Salvador Bernabéu Albert. Consejo Superior de Investigaciones Científicas, 2009.

Pacheco Rojas, José de la Cruz. "Sistema misional y cambio cultural en el noroeste novohispano." In *Los jesuitas en el norte de Nueva España: Sus contribuciones a la educación y el sistema misional,* edited by José de la Cruz Pacheco Rojas. Universidad Juárez del Estado de Durango, 2004.

Paz Frayre, Miguel Ángel. "La Compañía de Jesús y la conquista en el noroeste de la Nueva España." In *Antropología del desierto: Etnicidad e identidad,* edited by Rafael Pérez-Taylor, Itzkuauhtli Zamora Sáenz, and Carlos González Herrera. Universidad Nacional Autónoma de México, 2013.

Pennington, Campbell W. *The Tarahumar of Mexico: Their Environment and Material Culture.* University of Utah Press, 1963.

Pérez Alonso, Manuel Ignacio, ed. *La Compañía de Jesús en México: Cuatro siglos de labor cultural, 1572–1972.* Editorial Jus, 1972.

Pérez de Ribas, Andrés. *Triunfos de nuestra Santa Fe entre gentes las más bárbaras y fieras del nuevo orbe.* 3 vols. Layac, 1944.

Phillips, David A. "Arqueología de la Sierra Madre Occidental de Chihuahua." In *Actas del Segundo Congreso de Historia Regional Comparada 1990,* edited by Ricardo León García. Universidad Autónoma de Ciudad Juárez, 1991.

Polzer, Charles W. *The Evolution of the Jesuit Mission System in Northwestern New Spain, 1600–1767.* University of Arizona Press, 1972.

Polzer, Charles W. "Four Corridors to the Kingdom: Northern and Southern New Spain." In *The Gran Chichimeca: Essays on the Archaeology and Ethnohistory of Northern Mesoamerica,* edited by Jonathan E. Reyman. Ashgate, 1994.

Porras Muñoz, Guillermo. *La frontera con los indios de Nueva Vizcaya en el siglo XVII.* Fondo Cultural Banamex, 1980.

Porras Muñoz, Guillermo. *Iglesia y estado en Nueva Vizcaya, 1562–1821.* Universidad Nacional Autónoma de México, 1980.

Porras Muñoz, Guillermo. *El nuevo descubrimiento der San José del Parral.* Universidad Nacional Autónoma de México, 1988.

Powell, Philip W. *La guerra chichimeca, 1550–1600.* Translated by Juan José Utrilla. Fondo de Cultura Económica, 1985.

Quijada López, César Armando. "Las rebeliones indígenas y sus repercusiones en los Reales de Minas: San Juan Bautista, Sonora, un ejemplo." In *El noroeste de México: Sus culturas étnicas; Seminario de etnografía "Fernando Cámara Barbachano,"* edited by Donaciano Gutiérrez and Josefina Gutiérrez Tripp. Instituto Nacional de Antropología e Historia, 1991.

Reff, Daniel T. *Disease, Depopulation, and Culture Change in Northwestern New Spain, 1518–1764.* University of Utah Press, 1991.

Reff, Daniel T. *Plagues, Priests, and Demons: Sacred Narratives and the Rise of Christianity in the Old World and the New*. Cambridge University Press, 2005.

Rejón, Francisco. "El aporte teológico de la Compañía de Jesús y los problemas morales de las Indias: El caso de la esclavitud." In *Los jesuitas y la modernidad en Iberoamérica, 1549–1773*, vol. 1, edited by Manuel Marzal and Luis Bacigalupo. Fondo Editorial de la Pontificia Universidad Católica del Perú, 2007.

Reyes Landa, María Luisa. "Continuidad y cambio cultural en los grupos nómadas del Norte de Nueva Vizcaya." PhD diss., Universidad Michoacana de San Nicolás de Hidalgo, 2011.

Roberts, David. *The Pueblo Revolt: The Secret Rebellion That Drove the Spaniards out of the Southwest*. Simon & Schuster, 2004.

Rodríguez, Juan Luis. *La Sierra Tarahumara: Travesías y pensares*. Instituto Nacional de Antropología e Historia, 2008.

Rodríguez López, Abel. "El *Compendio de la Lengua Tarahumara* de 1683: Notas etnográficas sobre una micro región chichimeca, Alta Tarahumara, 1675–1683." In *Continuidad y fragmentación de la Gran Chichimeca*, edited by Andrés Fábregas Puig, Mario Alberto Nájera Espinoza, and Claudio Esteva Fabregat. Seminario Permanente de Estudios de la Gran Chichimeca, Universidad de Guadalajara, 2008.

Rodríguez López, Abel. "Paradigmas epistemológicos y la cultura rarámuri." In *La investigación antropológica y la formación profesional en el norte de México*, edited by Mónica Sofía Iturbide Robles. Escuela de Antropología e Historia del Norte de México, 2013.

Rodríguez-Sala, María Luisa, Ignacio Gómezgil R. S., and María Eugenia Cué. *Exploradores en el septentrión novohispano*. Miguel Ángel Porrúa, 1995.

Roedl, Bohumír. "La crónica de Joseph Neumann como fuente histórica." In *Historia de las sublevaciones indias en la Tarahumara*, edited by Bohumír Roedl and translated by Simmona Binková. Universidad Carolina, 1994.

Rubio Mañé, J. Ignacio. *El virreinato*. Vol. 2, *Expansión y defensa*. Part 1. Universidad Nacional Autónoma de México, 1983.

Rubio Mañé, J. Ignacio. *El virreinato*. Vol. 3, *Expansión y defensa*. Part 2. Universidad Nacional Autónoma de México, 1983.

Salmón, Roberto Mario. "Seventeenth Century Tarahumara: A History of Cultural Resistance." Master's thesis, University of New Mexico, 1975.

Saravia, Atanasio G. *Obras. Apuntes para la historia de la Nueva Vizcaya*. Vol 2. Universidad Nacional Autónoma de México, 1979.

Sariego Rodríguez, Juan Luis. "La antropología de la Tarahumara: Nuevos y viejos debates." In *Chihuahua Hoy 2005: Visiones de su historia, economía, política y cultura*, vol. 3, edited by Víctor Orozco. Universidad Autónoma de Ciudad Juárez, 2013.

Sariego Rodríguez, Juan Luis. "Chihuahua: El lugar donde la antropología llegó tarde." In *Antropología en las orillas*, edited by Victoria Novelo and Juan Luis Sariego. Universidad Intercultural de Chiapas, 2011.

Sariego Rodríguez, Juan Luis, ed. *El indigenismo en Chihuahua: Antología de textos.* Escuela Nacional de Antropología e Historia, Universidad de Chihuahua, 1998.

Sariego Rodríguez, Juan Luis. "El indigenismo en la Sierra Tarahumara." In *Continuidad y fragmentación de la Gran Chichimeca,* edited by Andrés Fábregas Puig, Mario Alberto Nájera Espinoza, and Claudio Esteva Fabregat. Seminario Permanente de Estudios de la Gran Chichimeca, Universidad de Guadalajara, 2008.

Servín Herrera, Loreley, and Aída Isela González. "Visiones y discursos sobre los rarámuri en la ciudad de Chihuahua." In *Imágenes del racismo en México,* edited by Alicia Castellanos Guerrero. Universidad Autónoma Metropolitana / Plaza y Valdés, 2003.

Silva Antonio, Gabriela. *Catálogo de documentos para la historia de las misiones: Documentos para la historia de las misiones del noroeste localizados en el Archivo Histórico de la Provincia Mexicana de la Compañía de Jesús.* Universidad Iberoamericana, El Colegio de Sinaloa, 2001.

Swann, Michael M. *Tierra Adentro: Settlement and Society in Colonial Durango.* Westview Press, 1982.

Vaca Cortés, Jesús. *Rarámuri: El lugar de la vida y la muerte.* Instituto Chihuahuense de la Cultura, 2003.

Valiñas Coalla, Leopoldo. "Lo que la lingüística yutoazteca podría aportar en la reconstrucción histórica del Norte de México." In *Nómadas y sedentarios en el norte de México: Homenaje a Beatriz Braniff,* edited by Marie-Areti Hers et al. Universidad Nacional Autónoma de México, 2000.

Vallebueno Garcinava, Miguel, and Antonio Reyes Valdez, eds. *Patrimonio misional en el sur de la Nueva Vizcaya.* Instituto Nacional de Antropología e Historia, 2009.

Villalpando Canchola, María Elisa. "Reducciones jesuitas del siglo XVII en las provincias costeras y Santa Bárbara de la Nueva Vizcaya." *Noroeste de México* 10 (1991): 19–30.

Waterhouse, Ewing. "A Jesuit Mission in the Sierra Tarahumara." *Journal of the Southwest* 45, no. 1–2 (Spring–Summer 2003): 63–86.

Zavala, Silvio A. *Las instituciones jurídicas en la conquista de América.* Editorial Porrúa, 1988.

INDEX

Page numbers in italics refer to figures, maps, or tables.

ABOUT THE AUTHOR

Joseph P. Sánchez is founder and former director of the Spanish Colonial Research Center at the University of New Mexico. He retired from the National Park Service (NPS) in 2014 after thirty-five years of service. From 2003 to 2014 he served as superintendent of Petroglyph National Monument. Before his career with NPS, he was a professor of colonial Mexican history and director of the Mexican American Studies and Research Center at the University of Arizona, Tucson. He has taught at the University of New Mexico, Santa Ana College in California, and the Universidad Autónoma de Guadalajara, Mexico, and he has published several studies on Spanish frontiers in California, Arizona, New Mexico, Texas, and Alaska. He is the author of several books, including *Pueblos, Plains, and Province: New Mexico in the Seventeenth Century*.